Cubism and Fashion

Cubism
and
Fashion

Richard Martin

The Metropolitan Museum of Art

Distributed by Harry N. Abrams, Inc., New York

This volume has been published in conjunction with the exhibition "Cubism and Fashion," held at The Metropolitan Museum of Art from December 10, 1998, through March 14, 1999.

The exhibition is made possible by **PRADA**.

Published by The Metropolitan Museum of Art, New York

John P. O'Neill, Editor in Chief
Barbara Cavaliere, Editor
Design by Matsumoto Incorporated, New York
Rich Bonk, Production

Library of Congress Cataloging-in-Publication Data

Martin, Richard
    Cubism and fashion / Richard Martin
        p.   cm.
    Accompanying an exhibition to be held at The Metropolitan Museum of Art from December 10, 1998, to March 14, 1999.
        ISBN 0-87099-888-9. — ISBN 0-8109-6532-1 (Abrams)
    1. Fashion—History—20th Century—Exhibitions. 2. Costume design—History—20th century—Exhibitions. 3. Cubism—Influence—Exhibitions. I. Metropolitan Museum of Art (New York, N.Y.) II. Title.
    TT502.M3684   1998
    746.9'2'0904—DC21
98-44882

CIP

All works by Georges Braque, Albert Gleizes, Fernand Léger are:
© 1998 Artists Rights Society (ARS), New York / ADAGP, París

All works by Marcel Duchamp are:
© 1998 Artists Rights Society (ARS), New York / ADAGP, París / Estate of Marcel Duchamp

All works by Henri Matisse are:
© 1998 Succession H. Matisse, Paris / Artists Rights Society (ARS), New York

All works by Pablo Picasso are:
© 1998 Estate of Pablo Picasso / Artists Rights Society (ARS), New York

All works by Robert and Sonia Delaunay are:
© L & M SERVICES B.V. amsterdam 981104

The credit line and/or copyright notice for photographs of works of art that have been provided by various sources appear under each illustration.

The costume photography in this volume is by Karin L. Willis, The Photograph Studio, The Metropolitan Museum of Art.

Unless otherwise indicated, the costumes in this volume are in the collection of The Costume Institute, The Metropolitan Museum of Art. The illustrations on the cover and on pages 130 to 142 are in the collection of the Irene Lewisohn Library, The Costume Institute.

Color separations by Professional Graphics, Rockford, Illinois
Printed by Julio Soto Impresor, S.A., Madrid
Bound by Encuadernación Ramos, S.A., Madrid
Printing and binding coordinated by Ediciones El Viso, S.A., Madrid

Front cover: Thayaht, "L'Orage"
Robe by Madeleine Vionnet
Gazette du Bon Ton, 1923

Frontispiece: Pablo Picasso, *Woman Sewing*, 1909–10
Oil on canvas, 31 1/2 x 23 1/4 in. (80 x 59.1 cm)
Courtesy of Richard Gray Gallery, Chicago/New York

Contents

Foreword

"The 10's, the 20's, the 30's," two
Poiret dresses

I first became acquainted with Richard Martin's work through his book *Fashion and Surrealism* (1987). Disappointed at how inadequate most generalizing propositions attempting to equate or affiliate fashion with art had been, I welcomed in *Fashion and Surrealism* the focus and authority achieved by dealing with this subject through a specific example. Now I am happy to commend another analysis. This one recognizes the manifest, although hitherto unacknowledged, links between fashion and art, in this case Cubism. As Richard Martin argues, an unnamed revolution occurred in fashion during the critical years between about 1908 and the later 1920s; it saw three-dimensional forms, once of Belle Epoque amplitude and corseted and buttressed fortification, dissolve into flat planes, cylinders, and mutable forms suggesting abstraction rather than representation.

Twenty-five years ago this month, The Costume Institute presented one of its most intriguing and I'm afraid worst titled exhibitions, "The 10's, the 20's, the 30's: Inventive Clothes, 1909–1939." While its span is not squarely congruent with the thesis of "Cubism and Fashion," there is a considerable overlap. Perhaps there is something else as well. The 1973–74 exhibition aroused the interest of fashion designers and others in the work of Madeleine Vionnet, Callot Soeurs, and early Chanel. Richard Martin considers this show to be the most visionary exhibition mounted in The Costume Institute in the 1970s. After a quarter of a century, there now emerges a name for many of its salient and best features: Cubism and fashion. That is not to say that our current exhibition is in any way a recapitulation. On the contrary, it is a necessary reconsideration, one that brings a reason and an ordering to what we had long prized without name and without analytical explication.

Robert Rosenblum has best understood the "magnanimity" of Cubism, realizing in his landmark book *Cubism and Twentieth-Century Art* (1960) that Cubism, born of a radical new vision, is yet the quiet reformation of twentieth-century sight, offering decades of fresh, fascinating options. It has taken us nearly nine decades to dare to say that Cubism has been a compelling force in fashion, even if we ourselves inadvertently offered that evidence twenty-five years ago. So it is that we learn from art, sometimes by immediate revelation, sometimes by slowly unfolding truth.

The Museum gratefully acknowledges the assistance provided by Prada toward the exhibition.

Philippe de Montebello
Director
The Metropolitan Museum of Art

Top to bottom
"The 10's, the 20's, the 30's," four Vionnet dresses
"The 10's, the 20's, the 30's," three Poiret ensembles
"The 10's, the 20's, the 30's," two Vionnet dresses

Top to bottom
"The 10's, the 20's, the 30's," three Chanel dresses
"The 10's, the 20's, the 30's," Molyneux, Vionnet, and Grès dresses
"The 10's, the 20's, the 30's," three white Vionnet dreses, Grès second from right

Introduction

Cubism and Fashion is an attempt to understand the fundamental changes in fashion that occurred between about 1908 and about 1925 and to offer the proposition that perhaps Cubism, which transfigured art so fundamentally during that epoch, is also a prime cause of fashion's modern forms. Of course, such a proposition is viable only if the aesthetic principle is viewed openly and construed as broadly applicable. Cubism is incontestably broad-minded, inasmuch as like that later "ism," Surrealism, its reform was in large part about diminishing the privileges of painting and sculpture and honoring the values of the ordinary. It was almost inevitable that the planes, cylinders, mutable optics, and dynamic motion of Cubist art would engage fashion. Art historians have seen phenomena as diverse as air travel and the Theory of Relativity as akin— if not kin—to Cubism's invention of a new way of seeing. In the search for a description of or analysis for fashion's radical transformation, it becomes clear that Cubism possesses both the aesthetic proximity and the worldly diffusion to be not only metaphor but also cause.

Unquestionably, elements of fashion's transfiguration have social causes—most notably the new physical mobility of automobiles and the accompanying palpability of speed as well as the cultural ascent of women—but social causes alone are insufficient to explain the scale of the changed perceptions involved. *Garçonnes*, liberated and enfranchised women, and sports participants can all be imagined wearing the garments that you see in this book, but their enumeration alone cannot account for the transfiguration. Rather, it was that remarkable aesthetic reversal of Cubism that deflated the Renaissance optics of Alberti and Giotto to render for modern art options in flatness and the plane that might also explain modern fashion, especially in the absence of any other sufficient reason.

Like Surrealism, Cubism—at its core—lacks pretense. Art it is, yet never is it striving art, pompous or affected. As Rosalind Krauss has recently argued in *The Picasso Papers*, the new configurations were open to many views, filled with the ordinary and the deliberately non-aesthetic, and rendered by artists both tentative and as magisterial as Picasso. Fashion answered to the sensibility of Cubism almost immediately and consistently through the 1910s and 1920s, but it is not that fashion was seeking art's fine privileges, for Cubism was disavowing those very privileges. Fashion took on the principles of Cubism long before Cubism had become the Establishment. It cannot be said that fashion arrayed itself in the cloak of Cubism as a sanctuary. Rather, fashion aligned itself with Cubism when that new art was still enterprise, innovation, and adventure. Of course, we still feel risk and wonder when we see the unadorned ligatures of lines and planes in a Vionnet dress or the versatility of tailored outfits that are indeterminate in parts and functions yet project a willful determination to be modern.

The fashion transfiguration of which I speak is no small matter. It is crucial to modern fashion; it is a way of seeing and making that goes far beyond one season's alterations in color or silhouette. It can be modestly but rightly stated: Cubism and fashion.

Top to bottom
"The 10's, the 20's, the 30's," three Vionnet dresses
"The 10's, the 20's, the 30's," four Callot Soeurs dresses
"The 10's, the 20's, the 30's," three Poiret ensembles

From Three Dimensions to Two

Madeleine Vionnet

Day dress (detail), 1926–27

Maroon silk crêpe

Gift of Mrs. Aline Bernstein, 1945

(CI 45.103.2)

An intersection of pin-tucked seams functions both as fragmenting line and assembling structure in this Vionnet dress. Nothing more, or less, gives shape in this soft dress, in which the pin tucking provides the transition between an uninflected bias bodice and a box-pleated skirt. The delicate lattice is the essential structure of the dress, gibing all form and shape. Of course, it exemplifies form as function, a modern tenet seldom tested against but paramount in Vionnet.

In the years from about 1908 through the 1920s, fashion moved from the statuesque to the soft and supple. In one generation, or what could accountably be a short lifetime, fashion abandoned the bold, body-aggrandizing silhouette of the Belle Epoque and chose to believe in a soft cylinder that is hardly descriptive of the body within. Noteworthy, yet never before named, it is this transfiguration that we will call *Cubism and Fashion*, hoping that crossing back and forth between analysis of art and fashion—two arts pertaining to visions of the body, after all—we can better understand the profound change that occurred in fashion. With or without Cubism, how could one live through changes as dramatic as these in one generation. The twentieth century started with the kind of jolt that even an accomplished historian such as Henry Adams could not have imagined for the century of the dynamo.

After all, fashion had long been secure in the hyperbolic body of the woman. Since the 1830s at least, there had been a steady practice to create around a harmonic set of proportions of the human body, occasionally squeezing a little, largely adding strategically. After seventy years that had seen crinolines and bustles come and go, there was no reason to think that the varying pneumatics of body enhancement in clothing might not safely continue for another seven or eight decades. What we see at the beginning of this chapter through the fortified grandeur of House of Worth dresses is the fulfillment of such principles. One could have imagined that those immense upper sleeves might have deflated and another body part might have shifted in relative shape or size. Why did the time-honored process suddenly end and the entire body change? There is, as in the transfiguration that happened between the 1780s and 1810, no major social revolution such as democracy to explain the emergence of a neoclassical style. And that explanation seems simple compared to what happened around 1908.

We could argue that it is the art of Cubism and a specific, if never codified, suite of aesthetic principles that changed the world of fashion. Both more plausible and more practical is the likelihood that it was not the art of Cubism per se but the culture of Cubism that influenced fashion, just as the culture of Cubism might be said to align it with new ideas in theater, literature, and eventually, the movies. Cubism was never rarefied; it insisted on an art less remote and supreme than before. Art historians who have deftly defined the culture of Cubism have been famous for their slides of equations and physics and their suggestions that Cubist mass is dynamic and relative; others show flat landscapes seen aerially to demonstrate that air flights performed in 1903 and the dynamics of space in Cubism are visually alike. Indeed, we have attributed a culture to Cubism, whether the art is root cause or not.

To melt the obdurate silhouette is one achievement of those critical years. To disintegrate the forms of dress, allowing for multiple readings and ambiguities, is another. Like the dislocations of focus and the new lack of surety in perspective, fashion underwent a similar reformation in several stages. The flat overlaps that replaced the architectonics in wardrobe established planes in uncertain relationships. At times, we do not know what underlaps and what overlaps. Further, in dresses by Vionnet, Chanel, and others, the new segments that form the garment are all of equal importance, causing the eye to flicker among the various fragments. In short, the same indeterminacy of forms that Cubism fostered in painting, sculpture, and collage obtains in fashion during the same years of innovation, albeit fashion's process is more attenuated.

It is essential to recognize that Cubism in fashion did not merely dethrone the magnitude and representational paradigm of the Belle Epoque silhouette but that it offered in fashion, as in art, a substantive and new manner of seeing, reasoned in dynamics of time and space, rendered with the volatility of modern life. Although it could be mistaken as late as the Armory Show in America in 1913 as an incomprehensible, unaccountable pure abstraction, Cubism was nonetheless a systematic process of seeing. For fashion, dynamic lines realized on the flat plane could be the equivalent of pattern pieces, and the process of design in two dimensions through draping could be a parallel to Cubism's affirmation of the planar probity of art. Fashion could, in fact, even serve as a kind of proof of the viability of Cubism: the Cubist aesthetic in fashion had to allow for movement and the workable surround of a three-dimensional human being, even while it expressed the forms of Cubism. Thus, a sports ensemble attributed to

Jean Patou (pages 38–39) makes apparel into a set of flat designs, but it can be so only when sufficient flexure for the body within is allowed and when the linear enterprise of the top, apparently an abstraction, works its way into the pleats of the skirt, which are compatible with the abstraction but function as pure clothing operations, not as an abstraction. All design is sublimated into the garment, including the regular tucks that form the neckline.

But it is collage, so central to the invention of Cubism, that is most revealed as the paradigm for the new decoration in sheer, collapsed, transparent forms that takes the place of bulky, space-assuming, representation-seeking forms of the earlier three-dimensional silhouette. Examples in this chapter from as early as 1910 and the years before the First World War indicate that designers as diverse as Callot Soeurs and Lucile accepted the challenge of multiplicity realized on the plane as opposed to the deep realms of dress when troughs and folds and extensions model the body into mass. Eschewing mass, these designers created with the delicacy of collage and its unsure veneers and minor spatial intervals just as surely as the artists of collage had in the months and years before them. It could only be an act of faith in the new to be able to wear a garment that so affirmed the fragile plane, that so advanced the new aesthetic and culture of Cubism.

Georges Seurat
Study for "A Sunday on La Grande Jatte," 1884
Oil on canvas, 27 ³/₄ x 41 in.
(70.5 x 104.1 cm)
The Metropolitan Museum of Art,
New York
Bequest of Sam A. Lewisohn, 1951
(51.112.6)

Seurat's tableau of robust figures, their
silhouettes determined by body-shaping
garments, is perceived as scenographic
space inhabited by figures of
representational dimensions and account.
Like an 1880s dress, the painting is a
simulation of three-dimensional form, even
as Seurat's Pointillist flecking draws our
attention toward the surface. Form is yet as
fabricated and inflated as it is in the Worth
bridal gown shown on pages 19 to 21. This
is hyperbolic three-dimensionality.

Jean-Philippe Worth
Wedding gown (and details), 1896
Cream silk damask
Gift of Miss Agnes Miles Carpenter, 1941
(CI 41.14.1)

The bulbous balloon of an upper sleeve contrasts with a tight wrist and slender forearm. Tuba and piccolo in an orchestra, sweet and sour on the palate—such declarations of maximum range were part of the virtuoso achievement and repertoire of tricks of the house of Worth in the 1890s. An upholstered torso, breathlessly tight waist, and buttressed hips leading into a bell shape defined a Worth body, but with the flair of the same fabric bursting out in big upper sleeves and gracefully tapering forearms. Worth represented the body grandly, even grandiloquently; everything that he offered was his version of the perfect body. It was this world that Cubism in fashion sought to reject.

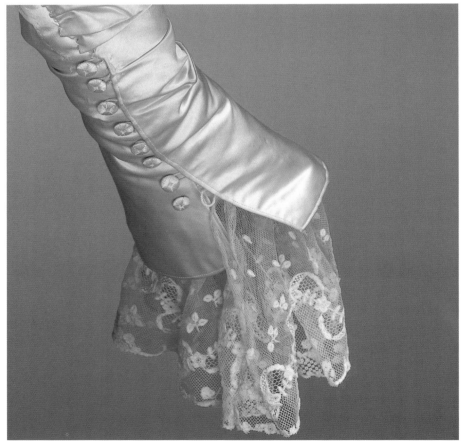

Pablo Picasso

Les Demoiselles d'Avignon, July 1907
Oil on canvas, 96 x 92 in.
(243.9 x 233.7 cm)
The Museum of Modern Art, New York
Acquired through the Lillie P. Bliss
Bequest

Display and enticement are no longer
three-dimensional and subject to a
Renaissance spatial grid. The body is no
longer an integer, but it is capable of being
fragmented, seen multiplely, and put into
motion. On the facing page, a Callot
Soeurs dress assumes a similar new space
and freedom from the conventions of the
primacy of volume. In both instances, the
body is enhanced by being flattened. In
the withering of the three-dimensional
forms of bodies and of apparel parts,
Cubism offers the effectively nimble
weightlessness of a buoyant ensemble,
whether pictorial or wardrobe.

Callot Soeurs

Evening dress (and detail of skirt), ca. 1926
Pieced green, gray, and pink silk faille embroi-
dered with polychrome and metallic thread and
green silk moiré with overlay of metallic lace
Gift of Mrs. John Magnin, 1940 (CI 40.4)

Whereas the ponderous creations of the
Belle Epoque allowed for both layers of
accretions and a deep stratification of the
interior, the dresses of Callot Soeurs are as
flat as a pancake. What layering exists is
wafer thin and composed of unflanged arcs
and crescents of sheer overlay. Still of an
older order in not eschewing ornament,
the Callot Soeurs worked ornament subject
to the plane. Amplification and accretion
were deliberately avoided. Moreover, in the
construction of this particular garment, the
fabric is pieced and thereby worked by
abutments, not by overlap or layering.
That method is discernible in the obdurate
flatness, never allowing for protrusion,
curl, or even heavy seam of fabric.

Left:

Charles Frederick Worth

Ball gown, ca. 1887
Pale green and ivory silk satin, and yellow,
pink, and ivory silk chiffon with embroidered
sunburst pattern
Gift of Orme Wilson and R. Thornton
Wilson, in memory of their mother,
Mrs. Caroline Schermerhorn Astor Wilson,
1949 (49.3.28a, b)

Right (and detail on page 25):

Charles Frederick Worth

Ball gown, ca. 1892
Pink silk damask with crystal embroidery
Gift of Orme Wilson and R. Thornton
Wilson, in memory of their mother,
Mrs. Caroline Schermerhorn Astor Wilson,
1949 (CI 49.3.25a, b)

In the tradition of the second half of the nineteenth century, these gowns are heavily encrusted in decoration. The effect is not, however, to create a single sugary outer layer suggestive of a confection basted with sweetness and meant to have a unified crust. Rather, the effect is to accrue the utmost three-dimensionality, the never-give-up Christmas tree effect often pursued to the point of exhaustion or depletion of balls, tinsel, and other ornaments. Moreover, Charles Frederick Worth's long couture career suggests that the designer was chiefly interested in silhouette. More a sculptor than a painter, his disposition to ornament was equally three-dimensional: chenille fringe, passementerie, swansdown and fur trims, jet, pendant stones, and other fat and outsized forms were favorites, establishing the principle of decoration by animated, dangling, protruding, swaying, and extravagant ornament. Amplification and accretion were prized. Every impulse was to extend; it would have been anathema to suffer the flat plane.

Callot Soeurs

Evening gown (and detail), 1910–14
Beige cotton net embroidered with gold, silver,
pink, and copper sequins and beads
Gift of Jacqueline Loewe Fowler Costume
Collection, 1981 (1981.380.2)

Speaking of her training at Callot Soeurs, Madeleine Vionnet coyly commended its quality, saying, "Without the example of the Callot Soeurs, I would have continued to make Fords. It is because of them that I have been able to make Rolls Royces." Indeed, this is faint and self-serving praise, given that Callot Soeurs established the flatness of the plane on which Vionnet exercised the twist of bias and the weightless shifts of line. Without Callot Soeurs' tunics and soft dresses of the 1910s and 1920s, Vionnet's innovations are unimaginable.

In this decisive example, the Belle Epoque silhouette has collapsed into a cylinder of insubstantial cotton net incapable of standing up by itself. It would have always been believable that a Worth dress of the 1890s (see pages 24–25) could stand up by itself. Given the complete swoon from solid form to the melted and from freestanding to dependent form, we must acknowledge the transformation from an integrated, solid representation of the body (or its simulated, preferred modification) to a disintegrated abstraction based in flatness, the cylinder, and aesthetic contingencies. Assumed verisimilitude is replaced by adherence to abstract principles of dress. The boldness of the innovation of the Callot Soeurs is especially evident in the applied ornament. Sequins are confined to a flat plane on the net, even as they are spread in a regular overlap. They do not jut out or dangle (for there would be no sufficient substance or cantilever of dress architecture from which to suspend). Rather, their weighty skin applies its pressure back onto the already vulnerable net, causing it to fall more clingingly and conditionally on the body.

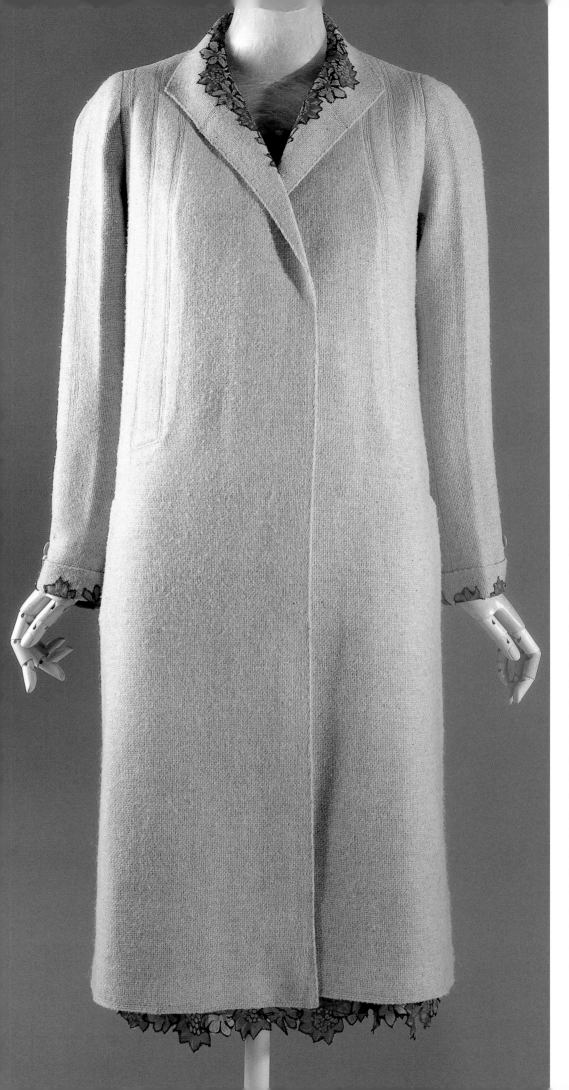

Gabrielle Chanel

Day ensemble (and details), ca. 1927
Pink and black floral-printed silk chiffon and
beige wool tweed
Isabel Shults Fund, 1984 (1984.31a–c)

Cubism's evisceration of conventional
representation has its direct counterpart in
this Chanel ensemble that denies every
accustomed ply of apparel material and
forms to achieve an overriding unity of
deflated, newly essentialized textile.
Through the 1920s and much of the 1930s,
Chanel avoided three-dimensional shapes
and favored their more two-dimensional
counterparts. Thus, the source of the
famous Chanel suit is not, in fact,
menswear tailoring in three dimensions.
It is the droopy and amorphous cardigan in
two dimensions, flexible enough to cover
and wrap but essentially a flat form.
Sportswear knits could invoke only the flat
and the possibility of the cylinder, but they
were definitely not molds stretched and
fitting on the body. In this ensemble, the
silk chiffon of the dress invades the tweed

coat, not in its entirety as a textile but
rather as individual flowers. As soft as the
fabric is, it is rendered even more pliable
when individual flowers are articulated. By
this process, the outermost stratum of
tweed—which we associate with the robust
and forceful—is invaded by the soft plane
of the dress. But the dress is also
susceptible to the same kind of adulteration
of its integrity as is a plane. At hem and
neckline, the material of the dress is
punctured and pieced to handstitched
individual flowers, to eliminate the fabric
in the interstices, letting flesh show
through at the neckline. This is a
deliberate insubstantiation, denying the
solidness of the dress just as resolutely as
Chanel denies the autonomy of the tweed
coat. Dematerializing textile into collage,
plying both inner and outer layers,
unifying soft and hard, Chanel is surely
practicing Cubism in fashion.

Juan Gris

Figure of a Woman, 1917
Oil on canvas (1.16 x .73 m)
Private Collection, Basel, Switzerland
Copyright Giraudon/Art Resource,
New York

Great expanses of flat planes in their airy
layerings suggest the entirety of the art of
Cubism as a creation in planes. Visibility
from one layer to another is not only
possible, it is the primary effect. Likewise,
for the Chanel ensemble on pages 28 to 30,
transparency is not a late affectation but a
property inherent to the work and its
delicate buildup of planes.

Georges Braque

Violin and Pitcher, 1910

Oil on canvas, 46 x 28 ³/₄ in.

(117 x 73 cm)

Kunstmuseum Basel

Copyright Giraudon/Art Resource,

New York

Cubism excited an uncertainty, its forms not wholly and specifically depicting but instead alluding to and offering traces of identity, even in the intense familiarity that characterizes still-life painting. One feels one's way successively through Cubist recognitions. So, too, these perceptions occur through the flattened elements of Cubist dress: one discriminates one layer; one discovers a floral motif; one even extrapolates other strata less distinct. The indeterminacy and the discoveries come to be the delight of the work.

Lucile

Evening dress (and detail of bodice), ca. 1916
Cream silk marquisette, cream cotton lace, and
light-blue silk satin
Gift of Julia B. Henry, 1978 (1978.288.1a, b)

Although she had an old-fashioned
sensibility for the feminine that defined
waists in belts and cummerbunds in
otherwise cylindrical silhouettes, Lucile
was modern in her use of tissue-thin
layerings and veilings. A modern-day
Salome has to be envisioned in these
dresses. Even with small folds and satin
flower buds, the effect is to enhance the
surface, to make the dress function as a flat
plane as if in a collage, in which shifting
transparencies and layers create a seductive
whole. Net can function for Lucile as chair
caning does for Picasso. The detail at left
indicates, though, how far removed this
collage culture in modern dress is from the
profligate pendant decoration of a decade
or two earlier. If lingerie dressing was and
has always been a modern impulse, Lucile
managed to create its most conservative
and proper version. Flaying away
clothing's obdurate body definitions and
arriving at a minimum of layers, lingerie
dressing always dances its seductive dance
of visibility: a fragment here, a fractured
plane there, an intimation of body then,
and a sheer, planar composition now,
much like Cubism.

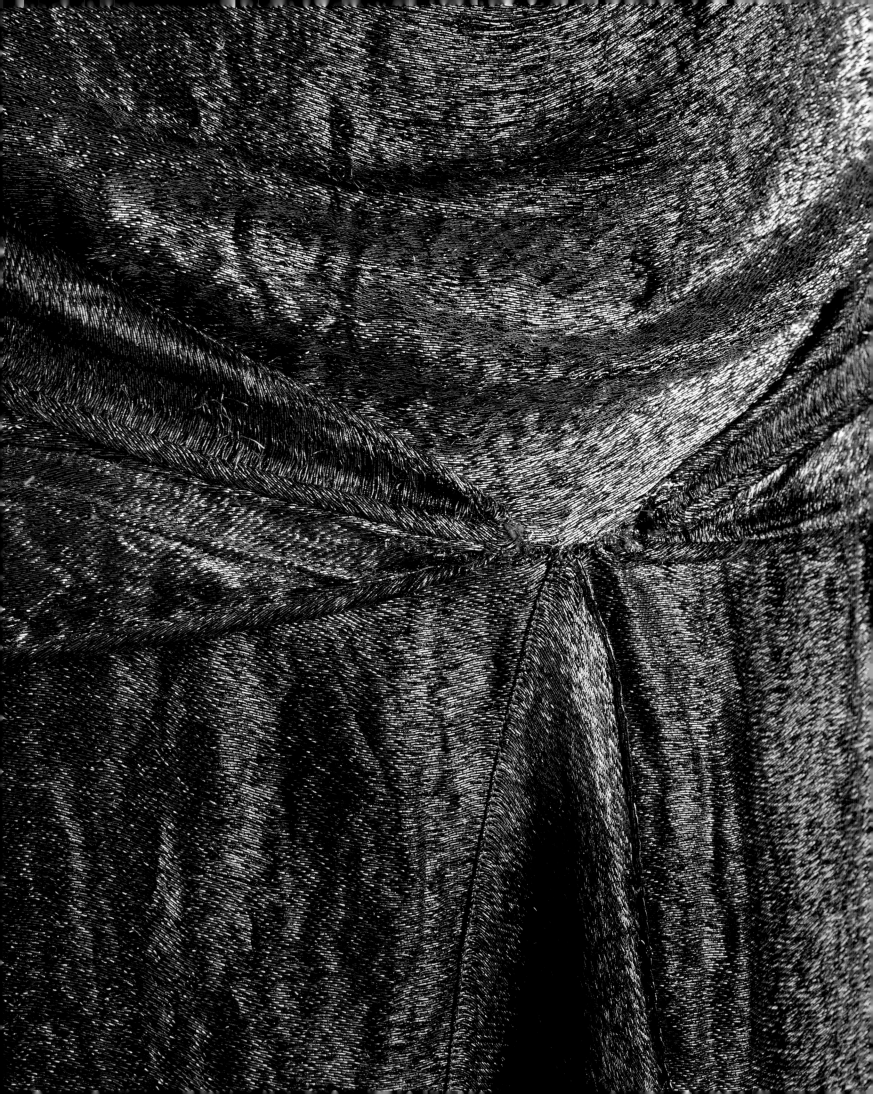

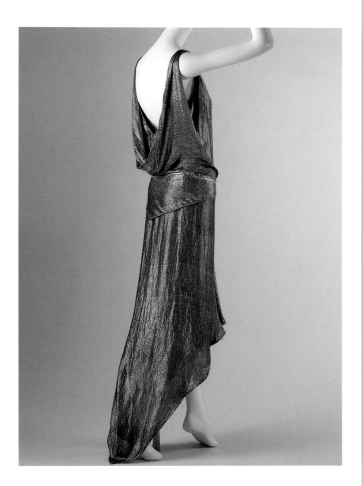

American

Evening dress and detail, ca. 1928
Compound weave of silver and gold
metallic thread
Gift of Mrs. Morton E. Snellenburg, 1946
(CI 46.46.3)

When earlier dresses were composed of
pattern pieces that approximated the
structure of the body, there was a tacit
understanding that shape was imparted to
apparel as a function of its responsibility to
the body. What, then, is the shaping
principle in the 1920s? One can see that it
is an abstraction of planes as they befit the
body. This example is probably an
American copy after an original by Leneif,
an important house in Paris in the 1920s,
when Leneif went on his own after
working for Poiret. Gold cloth reverses to
silver; a cowl effect at the back of the
bodice has points meeting at center-front
waist; a bias panel of silver is inset in the
front skirt; and a triangular silver girdle
pointing center-back is sewn to the waist.

Pablo Picasso

Dance of the Veils, 1907
Oil on canvas, 59 $^7/_8$ x 39 $^3/_4$ in.
(152 x 101 cm)
Hermitage State Museum, St. Petersburg
Copyright Scala/Art Resource,
New York

Through a metaphor of apparel, this
Picasso suggests the palpable presence of
the body, but that suggestion is spliced
over with wings of uncertain shape and
substance (the veils). As we know, some
found the obscured image indecipherable
in early paintings such as this one,
though we now see the forms distinctly.
For Picasso, the veils could be a
metaphor; in apparel, planes and veils
literally animate the body.

Fernand Léger
Femme en rouge et vert, 1914
Oil on canvas, 39 3/8 x 31 7/8 in.
(100 x 81 cm)
Collections Mnam/Cci—
Centre Georges Pompidou, Paris
Copyright Giraudon/Art Resource,
New York

Great cylinders of red and blue—almost
like bolts of cloth—roil through space to
create the equivalence of a human body. As
the dynamic course of geometry unfolds to
render the body, so, too, the geometry of
textile is disclosed on the human body in
fashion.

Paul Poiret

Evening dress, ca. 1920
Navy-blue and red silk faille
Gift of Mrs. Muriel Draper, 1943
(CI 43.85.2a, b)

In this visionary dress by Poiret, based on a yard-square poncho as its bodice inflected only by the modest cut of a bateau neckline, a geometric form is placed on the body, letting its cling (the silk faille is likely to cleave to the body) reconcile body and square. One could perceive the figure in this dress as a perfect ancient Roman Vitruvian man or an equally perfect twentieth-century Poiret woman, but a number of later alterations to snaps, buttons, and fasteners make it impossible to understand how this garment was originally worn or planned to be worn. At best, it can be seen as an anticipation of Issey Miyake's transfigurations of geometry in the 1970s and 1980s. Poiret is said to have referred to this as his "14 July dress," a more pedestrian citation. If Poiret's disposition was seldom geared to pure geometry, his interest in transforming the flat into the three-dimensional was evident in and informed by knowledge of Chinese, Japanese, and Middle-Eastern dress, especially the caftan and kimono to which this dress is chiefly indebted. Alice Mackrell, in *Paul Poiret* (London, 1990), published a similar or the same dress, claiming that it can be "arranged any way the wearer wishes."

Attributed to Jean Patou
Day ensemble (and detail), ca. 1927
Knitted cream and yellow silk
Purchase 1998

A rich vocabulary of forms derived from the arrow, vector, quill, chevron, and line into box pleat is incorporated into this sports outfit of the 1920s, in the quality and manner of Jean Patou, though without label or documentation. Patou, as importantly as Chanel but with far less recognition, advanced and promoted the knits and sweater dressing of sportswear style immediately after the First World War. Ironically, Patou had planned to show his first collection in 1914 but was interrupted by the War, in which he subsequently served. By 1919, he had presumably revised his silhouette to offer the first glimpses of a supple, leggy but dignified sportswear that would become his distinction. Such soft dressing was literally superficial, stressing a piece veneer using a decorative vocabulary strategically, suggesting dynamic motion through angled lines.

Jean Patou

Evening dress, ca. 1927
Off-white silk charmeuse embroidered with
colored beads and gold sequins
Gift of Mrs. John A. van Beuren and
Mrs. Samuel M. V. Hamilton, 1977
(1977.210.16)

If Chanel was the formidable figure of
sportswear, even in the 1920s and 1930s,
Patou was sportswear's gentleman, always
said to be debonair and a charmer. His
dresses exude such a winning confidence
and allure: an evening dress, for example,
has the simple silhouette of a tennis dress,
but it also has the kaleidoscopic beadwork
that is all but Fabergé in fantasy and also
extravagant in imagination. The armature
of the dress is as simple and as flat as
possible. As he had brought American
models to Paris to show his clothing, Patou
was indebted to the guileless all-American
girl as modern symbol, a quality correlative
to the artless modernism of his apparel.

Callot Soeurs

Day dress, ca. 1926
Lime-green silk embroidered with
polychrome silk floss
Gift of Mrs. John Chambers Hughes, 1958
(CI 58.34.11)

Skimming and subordinating the body, this
simple day dress by Callot Soeurs lets its
relative simplicity establish a field for a flat
decoration worthy of kimono or other
wrapped garment. Orientalism was
important to Callot Soeurs; imports and
expositions made it immensely popular
among Paris designers in the 1920s, and
Callot Soeurs had been among the first.
Cubism's influence is more conceptual and
provocative here than it is patternbook and
copyist. As art historian Robert Rosenblum
has noted, the many directions taken by
Cubism and its inspiration testify to its
largesse, not its laxity.

Callot Soeurs
Evening dress, ca. 1925
Green silk crêpe embroidered with
polychrome silk floss
Gift of Isabel Shults, 1944 (CI 44.64.12)

The Belle Epoque evening dress had been a formidable creature, readily anthropomorphized because she could stand up by herself. When in the closet, this dress must have looked almost exactly as when worn. By comparison, modern dress was no masquerade; the costume was limp or even slid to the floor in the closet, and it was only vested with power when worn. When flat, no longer specifically representational, and not as dogmatically single purpose as before, dress seems conjoined to the principles of Cubism.

Callot Soeurs

Lounging pajamas, ca. 1927

Yellow silk crêpe de chine printed with

polychrome pattern

Gift of Isabel Shults, 1944 (CI 44.64.19a–d)

While Poiret had established pantaloons and harem trousers as high-fashion options, especially in his gala "1002nd Night" ball, building on the Orientalist ideas of Amelia Bloomer's "Turkish trousers," designers in the 1920s took pajamas to the beach and to informal, at-home use. Of course, the barrier between leisure and formal dress was permeable in the 1910s and 1920s, as is evident in the emergence of the Fortuny tea gown into evening dress as well as in pajamas progression from boudoir to drawing room. Even to make pajamas would have been, a decade or two earlier, the fashion equivalent of making something as unprepossessing as a collage.

Georges Braque

Femme à la guitar, 1913
Oil on canvas, 51 ¹/₈ x 28 ³/₄ in.
(130 x 73 cm)
Collections Mnam/Cci—
Centre Georges Pompidou

Deriving its layers of form from the
medium of collage, Cubist representation
in paint is of intriguing complexity. Its tiers
are mutually related, but each is also a
layer and an object. Decoration for the
Cubist is perceptible as both whole and
part; the constituent parts have to be read
together through transparency and
relationships.

Callot Soeurs

Evening dress (and detail), ca. 1927
Peach silk, point d'esprit, gilt corded lace, and
pink and yellow silk satin ribbon rosettes
Gift of Martin Kamer, Switzerland, 1993
(1993.95)

Again and again, Callot Soeurs realized
layers that are so shimmery and sheer that
they hardly appear to be layers. The dress
achieves its conspicuous effect of flatness
because each layer is the lightest tissue in
juxtaposition to another and no single
stratum has any sense of weight or depth.
What is so remarkable here, as always,
about Callot Soeurs is that they offer an
abundance of decoration within the newly
leveled plane, just as much if not more than
one expected in full volumetric dresses of
decades earlier.

American or European
Evening dress, 1927–29
Blue silk velvet
Gift of Mrs. Arthur D. Pinkham, Jr., 1979
(1979.160.2)

The nonchalant drape—the slinkiness one
associates with the dance and evening attire
of the 1920s—of this velvet dress is
achieved by the balancing of big planes of
velvet rather like the fracturing of the
Cubist field. A like sense of the geometric
gives the dress a feeling of legerdemain,
never too heavy but with the weightless
suspension of the Cubist field no longer
gravity prone.

Paul Poiret

Evening gown, 1920s
Black silk chiffon brocaded with metallic
thread and black cotton net
Gift of Mrs. W. Allston Flagg, 1979
(1979.150.2)

The great innovations of Poiret had long
been abandoned as he struggled to stay in
business after World War I. The court
style of a 1920s gown would once have
been castigated as too conservative by the
self-proclaimed "King of Fashion," but
Poiret remained true to his interest in
setting any garment into the flat and the
sheer. Here, net and chiffon appear to
dissolve or disintegrate as too fragile to
maintain solid form. Of course, such a
figure in motion would be worthy of a
Duchamp or a Boccioni. The flicker and
flutter of motion animate the dress and the
movement of the body within.

Gabrielle Chanel

Day ensemble, 1926
Black wool jersey and silk satin
Purchase, Gift of New-York Historical Society,
by exchange, 1984 (1984.28a-c)

What is arguably the dress of the century
can be construed as economic reversal,
aesthetic purity, and practical manifesto.
The little black dress offers many
interpretations. Its planarity and
indeterminacy of form and function also
qualify it as a Cubist object.

Pablo Picasso
Three Women, 1907–8
Oil on canvas, 78 ³/₄ x 70 ¹/₈ in.
(200 x 178 cm)
Hermitage State Museum, St. Petersburg
Copyright ARS, New York

The interlocking of three women suggests
the particular power of Cubism to unify its
potential of imputed entanglement within
planes to suggest an intimacy like that of
the Three Graces. The shared vocabulary
of forms, not portraying the human body
as sovereign integer, allows for a greater
sense of dovetailed correlation.

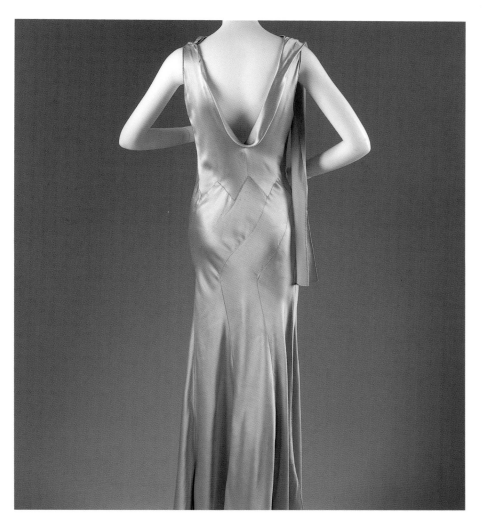

Madeleine Vionnet
Evening dress, ca. 1932
Pale-green silk charmeuse
Gift of Florence G. McAteer,
1982 (1982.422.8)

The pieces that enabled Vionnet to cover
the body in bias fabric, conjoined with the
straight grain, became a kind of origami of
sensuous shapes, especially as played off
against the body. The dynamic focus of the
dress is its construction, but construction
that is rendered both in the probity of line
and in the sensuous account of body
within. As in the Picasso on the facing
page, there is an interlocking pattern, but
there is a distinction among the planes. It
is, of course, the interlocking that
comprises the sole "decoration" of the
dress, thus positing ornament as inherent
in construction and as allowable only when
justified by construction.

The Analytical Art

Nemser, American or European
Day ensemble (detail), ca. 1926
Cream silk printed with geometric pattern in
shades of brown and brown melton wool
Gift of Richard Martin, 1998
(1998.235.5a, b)

Shown here is a detail of a Cubist-inspired ensemble composed of a dress and coat. Three views of the entire outfit are illustrated on pages 59 and 60.

Cubism is, by name and nature, analytical. So thorough was its departure from the traditional forms of representation that it almost had to justify its points of difference and distinction.

Cubism shattered the frozen moment of much Western representation and inculcated motion whenever possible. The forms and fragments that imply movement were everywhere, kinetic even when motion was not being charged. Among the fundamental affinities between fashion and Cubist art are the energy and the full spectrum from potential motion through energy released that are the imperatives of modern fashion. Clothing is not made for standing still, and fashion immediately took to Cubist theory and form that engaged movement. In some sense, few earlier art movements had been as promising and as tantalizing to fashion's innate and necessitous energy as Cubism was.

As ready as Futurism was to spring into action, Cubism was a perpetual motion machine, moving with every facet. For fashion, the energy was only exacerbated. A serene, rather bourgeois outfit (pages 56–57) by Jacques Doucet (who, after all, once owned Picasso's *Desmoiselles d'Avignon* [page 22] and could hardly be said to be ignorant of Cubism per se) waxes pure energy in its skirt panels that could easily swirl into the whirlwind of Boccioni's 1913 bronze sculpture *Unique Forms of Continuity in Space* and in its dynamic diagonals just above the waistline that carry that motion into the torso. The accompanying cape possesses its own bold and unusual animation: even more than a buccaneer's cape, this one suggests motion in its asymmetrical drape, playing against the diagonals that top the pleats of the skirt. The dynamic counterpart is equally present in the culture of Cubism, its energy and force finally becoming part of an equation with mass, not an intractable entity but a conditional ingredient, part of the larger recipe.

Cubism fostered indeterminacy of form, the ambiguities of space and motion. As the colossus of fashion's edifice crumbled and soft delineations prevailed, it was possible for the first time in decades to reconsider functional elements.

In one ensemble (pages 59–60), a scarf is no longer a complete thing in itself but has been incorporated into a coat. There is such a pairing and integration between the loose lining and the attached scarf that it is hard to describe whether the silk is scarf or lining. It has to become something more ambiguous and perhaps even indescribable. If the lining and the scarf have become a kind of Möbius continuum, so too even the dress has become an entity hard to parse despite its good common sense. Niches of pleats play against the fabric design throughout the skirt; everything about the dress seems to be in motion, and indeed it does suggest the excitement of motion. These energized fields are, of course, like the filled skies of Cubist landscapes that set clouds scuttling and the globe spinning; the propensity for analytical shapes puts every Cubist still-life into an energy field that slices every musical instrument and journal clipping as we move around and through the tabletop world. So, the observer of Cubist dress has to understand the presence of these changeable, indistinguishable forms as part of the unstoppable grace of the garment.

Of course, in Cubism the formal and the informal are reconciled. In the same ensemble from about 1927, a tailored coat and a silk dress are mutually responsive. Variant to a symphony of new instruments is the Louiseboulanger suit (pages 63–64) that undertakes Cubism in every explicit and implicit form. Stripes wrap; stripes serve to crenelate the tips of a scarf; pleats of a skirt transmogrify into a grid. Gestures of the soft fold betray the architectonics that venture beyond the tailored skirt and jacket into the wrap blouse and scarf. Here, the traditional divisions between dressmaking and tailoring have been obviated, as Cubism likewise ignores most of the categories in the fine arts. We will seldom see a blouse and scarf so precise and ready to be called tailored; we will not too often find suits so willing to yield to the soft blandishment that dressmaking promises. Correspondingly, the Doucet example works likewise for top and bottom.

This is innately tailoring's chapter in the history of Cubism. Couture dressmaking and other examples are included in relatively small number, but no other chapter in this book so fully addresses tailoring. Analytical Cubism in fashion is the fusion of tailoring and dressmaking, the occasion when the relatively crisp forms of suits and coats, along with stolid materials, are blended with the softer stuff in fashion. Transparency is seldom present to abet the planar function; here it is achieved through unerring, rigid line. But smart tailoring takes on the energy lines, the jagged jets of power, and the ambience of Cubism easily visually similar to that of the Cubist artists of Paris, who share with the fashion designers not only a city but also an intensity and dynamic energy.

As Robert Rosenblum has described of the first generation of Cubism in the fine arts, "For all the seeming solidity of this new world of building blocks, there is something strangely unstable and shifting in its appearance. The ostensible cubes of [Braque's] *Houses at L'Estaque* were to evolve into a pictorial language that rapidly discarded this preliminary reference to solid geometry and turned rather to a further exploration of an ever more ambiguous and fluctuating world." For fashion, a world that in its commercial sphere might not want to be advertised as "unstable and shifting," those principles prevail equally. Denying the straitjackets of clothing categories, allowing an apparel classification to migrate into new roles, and making us look carefully at clothing functions—these are all means for us to perceive and honor what Cubism brought: an indefinite new freedom, but a welcome and an unassailable freedom nonetheless.

Jacques Doucet

*Late-day ensemble (two views and detail),
1920–23*
*Rust wool, silk chiffon and crêpe embroidered
with clear and black beads*
Gift of Mrs. Olivia Constable, 1975
(1975.15a–c)

Suturing skirt and top with dynamic crests,
Doucet took the energetic emblems of
Cubism as the devices for fashion. Abstract
pattern makes sense on the figure only as a
demonstration of Cubist energy.
The cape's exaggerated asymmetry
(seen at right) affords an exciting
equilibrium, as does the dialogue between
the forms of the pleated skirt and the flat
blouse (seen above right).

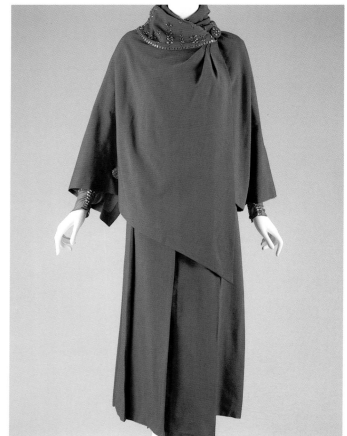

Marcel Duchamp
Nude Descending a Staircase No. 2, 1912
Oil on canvas, 58 x 35 in.
(147.3 x 88.9 cm)
Philadelphia Museum of Art: The Louise
and Walter Arensberg Collection

The singularity of the new motion, made
possible by stratified planes freed from
veristic depiction but nonetheless
demonstrative, produced an elegant energy,
a trait that could make much earlier
painting feel inert. One can imagine the
swing of a walking suit built out of
sympathetic parts moving in like harmony.

Nemser, American or European

Day ensemble (three views of dress and coat),
ca. 1926
Cream silk printed with geometric pattern in
shades of brown and brown melton wool
Gift of Richard Martin, 1998 (1998.235.5a, b)

Cubism's full complexities and
contradictions are seen in this chic 1920s
ensemble. As in Léger and Robert Delaunay,
the optic of Cubism has shifted here from
tabletop and collage to the city, its
architecture, and engineering. But the
principles of Cubism are also vested in
every stitch of the garment. With its
indeterminacy of form and multiple points
of view, the coat is alternatively architectonic
or swingingly loose. The scarflike
elongation of the lining is, in its way,
a hopeless hybrid, hard to understand as
either lining or scarf.

Fernand Léger
Le cirque, 1918
Oil on canvas, 25 $^5/_8$ x 21 $^1/_4$ in.
(65 x 54 cm)
Private Collection, Geneva
Copyright Giraudon/Art Resource,
New York

The circus, always transmitting an aura far
greater than the sum of its parts, exudes
animation rather than mere description.
Its cylinders and shapes imply excitement
and action, just as Cubist dress takes
advantage of clothing's inevitable
unfolding in motion.

Pablo Picasso
"Ma Jolie" (Woman with a Zither or Guitar),
1911–12
Oil on canvas, 39 $^3/_8$ x 25 $^3/_8$ in.
(100 x 65.4 cm)
The Museum of Modern Art, New York
Acquired through the Lillie P. Bliss
Bequest

Sleuthing in to find the body as palimpsest
beneath the warren of block and cubes, one
locates the figure, appearing as by magic
and with supreme clarity. For
corresponding suits and ensembles such as
the one on page 63, every layer both
betrays the body and portrays the body,
combining deceit and description,
chicanery and characterization.

Louiseboulanger

Suit (two views of jacket, skirt, blouse, and
scarf, and detail on next page), 1932
Ribbed knit blue wool and striped silk of cream,
blue, and gray
Gift of Miss Isabel Shults, 1944
(CI 44.64.25a–d)

The 1930s locution of a "smart suit" comes
to life in this Louiseboulanger ensemble.
This suit is smart enough to fold and
unfold and to alternate between loose and
structured: it is smart enough to be Cubist.
The versatility of the blouse underlies the
suit's mixed messages of precision and ease.

Pablo Picasso

Harlequin, 1915

Oil on canvas, 72 $^1/_4$ x 41 $^3/_8$ in.
(183.5 x 105.1 cm)

The Museum of Modern Art, New York

Acquired through the Lillie P. Bliss
Bequest

Picasso's harlequin—identified by costume
and circus atmosphere—is both
unmistakably vivid and the deceiving
shaman capable of transfiguration. As
Cubist dress relished its own
contradictions, it often took on the
harlequin's masque and duplicity, alike in
floating planes and ambiguous shapes.

Jean Paquin

Day suit (and detail), early 1930s
Pieced purple suede and wool
Gift of Miriam Whitney Coletti, 1985
(1985.364.5a–c)

Modern vectors, sharpened by the primacy
of the plane, cut not only into the skies and
tabletops of Cubist art but also into the
pattern pieces and shaping of apparel. This
occurs whether through the form-yielding
insets of Vionnet or, in tailoring, through
the forceful lines in this Paquin day suit
that is otherwise all but bereft of
decoration.

Robert Delaunay

The Eiffel Tower, 1910–11
Oil on canvas, 76 3/4 x 50 3/4 in.
(195 x 129 cm)
Kunstmuseum Basel
Photograph Giraudon/Art Resource,
New York

The urban landscape and fashion
emerged together under the gaze of the
boulevardier. Fittingly, their Cubist
connection, comprising a further union,
is that both are dynamic and possess a
seeming agitation, though we all know
that what at first appeared to be agitation
became a modern pictorial cogitation.

Fernand Léger
The Confidences, 1921
Oil on canvas, 36 ¹/₄ x 25 ⁵/₈ in.
(92 x 65 cm)
Private Collection, Paris
Copyright Giraudon/Art Resource,
New York

By the 1920s, the Cubist revolution
was not over, but the new pictorial
system was commonplace in both art and
dress. Solid citizens were perceived
through the lens of Cubism, and they
wore apparel in its style.

French or American
Day suit (two views), ca. 1918
Brown wool
Gift of Susan Myrick, Barbara M. Myers,
Elizabeth M. Wissler, 1993 (1993.287.2a-d)

The cylinder of both modern dress and
Cubism is rendered dynamic in the lines of
this day suit, which pleat, zigzag, and
outline forms as if the probity of drawing
and the propensity to line could never
quite leave the design. Such daywear of the
teens clearly indicates that later fashion
examples in a similar vein are not
responding to the Art Deco of the 1920s
and 1930s but rather are continuing a
tradition in which kinetic energy is
bestowed on tailored clothing's simple lines
and pleatings, energy which is arguably
necessary for motion and is definitely the
symbol of motion.

Robert Delaunay

Window, 1912
Oil on cardboard, 15 ³/₈ x 11 ⁵/₈ in.
(39 x 29.6 cm)
Collections Mnam/Cci—
Centre Georges Pompidou, Paris
Photograph Scala/Art Resource, New York

The metaphor of the window, longstanding
for conventional space and depiction,
became Cubist space and depiction for
Delaunay. Facets, twists, and pieces
replaced the accustomed view as fully in
painting as they did in the world of
Vionnet dresses. Vionnet used a reduced-
scale mannequin to manipulate cloth; it
was her "window," making the cloth work
in new ways but honoring the conventions
of draping as well.

Madeleine Vionnet

Day dress (and detail), ca. 1932
Gold silk crêpe de chine
Gift of Miss Isabel Shults, 1944
(CI 44.64.22a, b)

In his preface to Betty Kirke's monograph
on Vionnet, designer Issey Miyake
compared his first impression of Vionnet
dresses with his first view of the *Nike of
Samothrace*. The sculpture of body
transcendent, accomplished through
drapery and despite abbreviation, is an
evocative equivalent to Vionnet, whose
adaptation of cloth on the body is so
supple, clinging, and natural. A gold dress
is almost more an Ian Fleming "007"
fantasy than it is a conventional garment,
as the dress approximates a sheathing in
gold leaf with just a few curling sleeves
and junctures to suggest that dress and
body are almost one, but not quite.

Robert Delaunay
La Parisienne, 1913
Oil on canvas, 48 x 33 ⅝ in.
(122 x 85.5 cm)
Museo Thyssen-Bornemisza, Madrid

As Delaunay configured the woman of his
time in circuits and blocks of color, so those
women wore such color-block geometries.
That is not to say that one was literally
descriptive of the other but that the Cubist
geometries pervaded dress and art.

Caroline Reboux

Cape, 1920s

Pieced polychrome silk satin lined

in brown satin

Gift of Miss Isabel Shults, 1952 (CI 52.5.2)

Giant paratriangles of color form a cape with deliberate artistic reference. Multicolored capes began during or before the time of Old Testament Joseph; Reboux's color is purposely constrained. She achieved the crucial shape of the triangle—Brancusi's *Bird in Space* is also a triangle—for the cape on the body. Laid flat, the cape is of a slightly irregular and ungainly shape, but Reboux has us direct our reading to the configuration on the body and not on the plane.

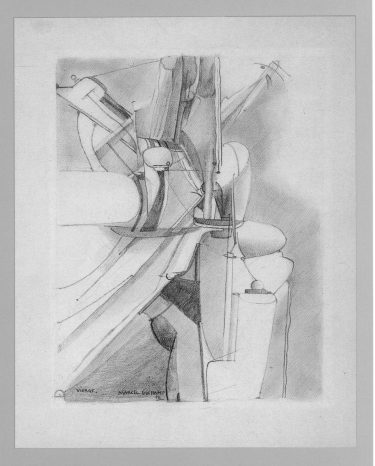

Madeleine Vionnet
Wedding dress (two views), 1929
Ivory silk panne velvet trimmed with
metallic cording
Gift of Mrs. van Heukelom Winn, 1974
(1974.261a–c)

There is no arsenic, but the new lace on a
1929 wedding dress is suggested by its
sectioning into shapes throughout its body
and train of more than seven feet. In fact,
there was an original lace veil, but here the
dress without veil is a triumph of linear
divisions made by the metallic cord.
Elegant rivers of form spread from one hip
or from the shoulder, their leaf-vein-like
separations through the train making it
seem even more elongated than it really is.

Marcel Duchamp
Bride, 1912
Oil on canvas, 35 ¹/₄ x 21 ⁷/₈ in.
(89.5 x 55.6 cm)
Philadelphia Museum of Art: The Louise
and Walter Arensberg Collection

If Duchamp's bride was very much the
graphic of a machine, Vionnet's later bride
was equally linear and elegant in the
manner of the Machine Age. Neither
seems a sentimental, blushing bride.

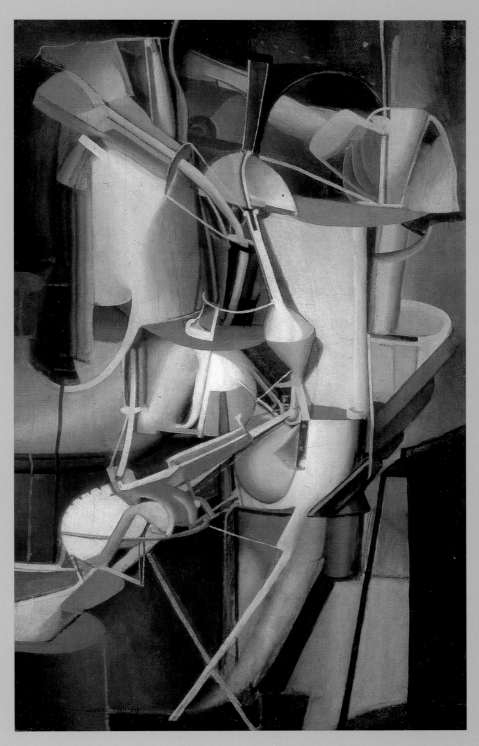

Marcel Duchamp
The Passage from Virgin to Bride, 1912
Oil on canvas, 23 ³/₈ x 21 ¹/₄ in.
(59.4 x 54 cm)
The Museum of Modern Art, New York,
Purchase

While the Duchampian mechanics are
fictive, they correspond to the problem-
solving rationalism of Vionnet's modern
wedding dress shown on pages 75 and 76.

Sonia Delaunay
La danseuse, 1916
Gouache on paper on glued cardboard,
11 $^5/_8$ x 10 $^7/_8$ in. (29.5 x 27.6 cm)
Collection Michel Seuphor, Paris
Photograph Giraudon/Art Resource,
New York

In a Cubist kaleidoscope of dance
notation, Sonia Delaunay captured both
motion and color, as they might
correspond to the triangular forms of a
cape in swirling movement such as the
one on page 79.

American

Evening coat, ca. 1914

Gold silk velvet trimmed with black dyed

Hudson Bay seal

Gift of Mrs. Carlo Vicario, 1948 (CI48.38.1)

As fashion became two-dimensional during the 1910s, fashion designers recognized that their new flatness was not like the tilt of the tabletop but a kimono flatness adjusted to a body wrapping. What reads as a triangle on the back of this evening coat is, of course, only a modified one with some curve to every side of the triangle.

Pablo Picasso
Woman with a Mandolin, 1909
Oil on canvas, 36 $^1/_4$ x 28 $^3/_4$ in.
(92 x 73 cm)
Hermitage State Museum,
St. Petersburg, Russia
Copyright Scala/Art Resource,
New York

Even as Picasso's planes of foreground and
background seem to dovetail, so too
Vionnet's supple but slight volumes and
junctures of front and back establish a
shallow space.

Madeleine Vionnet

Day dress, 1938
Beige silk crêpe
Gift of Mrs. Anthony Wilson, 1979
(1979.344.6)

While known for the drama of her evening
dresses, Vionnet is equally exceptional for
her day dresses in which the bias flutings
of silk, twists of form into volume, and
tricks of providing volume while skimming
across the body make her achievement
manifest. The malleable flutings of the
dress flicker and fracture with the same
variation as the optic with countless facets
in a Cubist painting.

Madeleine Vionnet
Day dress (and two details), ca. 1920
Ecru silk
Gift of Judith Backer Grunberg, 1993
(1993.228)

One of Vionnet's most triumphant dresses
carries the grand patterns of silk around
the body, while the fabric twists and tucks
back upon itself. The "subject" of this dress
is ultimately how it was made and how it
works as a composition. It is the fascination
of a Vionnet to recognize that the dress is,
in its way, transparent, yet it is also a kind
of three-dimensional, silk-swathing puzzle.

Georges Braque

Woman with Mandolin, 1910

Oil on canvas, 31 ³/₄ x 21 ¹/₄ in.

(80.5 x 54 cm)

Museo Thyssen-Bornemisza, Madrid

Copyright Nimatallah/Art Resource,

New York

The Cubists maintained the Romantic faith in synaesthesia, which professes that when looking at a painting of musical instruments, you can hear the music, in this case, of the mandolin. Interlocking blocks of form create figure and environment in the painting; in Vionnet such interlockings are twisted and tied.

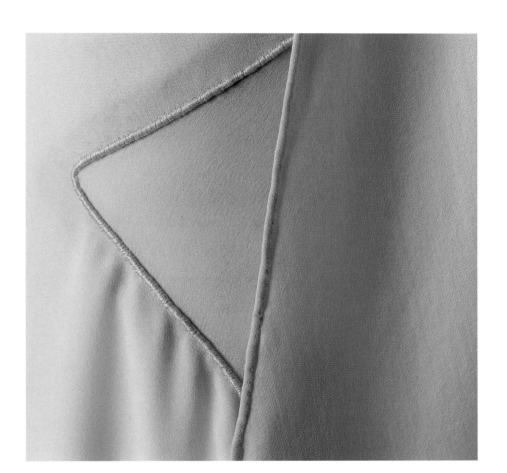

Fernand Léger

La Noce, 1911
Oil on canvas, 101 ¹/₈ x 81 in.
(257 x 206 cm)
Collections Mnam/Cci—Centre
Georges Pompidou, Paris
Copyright Giraudon/Art Resource,
New York

A whorl of energy brought to life out of
the Cubist vocabulary unifies the Léger
image, even as bands separate, but also
consolidate, a Chanel dress to the right.

Gabrielle Chanel

Evening dress (and detail), 1930s
Pink silk satin
Gift of Mrs. Maxime L. Hermanos, 1962
(CI 62.44.9a, b)

Arcing planes of satin define and
"decorate" this Chanel evening dress. Like
Chanel's gravity-defying tiers of lace, these
Cubist arcs sweep across the expected
structure of the dress to move around the
body, not in designated zones such as waist
or bust but in a gyroscope around the
body. She obviated the lateral slices that
traditonal fashion had required and
replaced them with a wondrous fruit-
peeling corkscrew that unifies the body
top to bottom.

Pattern and Collage

European

Two-piece ensemble (detail), ca. 1920
Red silk with polychrome appliqué
Gift of Mrs. Louis Rorimer, 1938
(CI 38.2.18a, b)

This detail of the costume illustrated on page 94 highlights the appliqué work on the brilliant red silk ensemble from about 1920.

Art historian Rosalind Krauss has suggested in poetic form the generation of the Picasso collage: "At first they seem to cycle through the crystal space like so many radiant facets of an absent jewel. Each newsprint fragment forms the sign for a visual meaning; then, as it butts against another, the sign re-forms and the meaning shifts." Of forms not at all fixed and of meaning not more fixed, the collage is always a wholly new creation made out of old, supposedly "known" elements. Making new the old as collage does, twentieth-century fashion sacrifices little other than the inflated volume of traditional dress. In almost all other aspects, fashion remains the same, but newly faceted and fitted into the planar model of what a new fashion might be.

Western fashion's index has always been the body that it concealed and more significantly that it described and analyzed. With Cubism, fashion was no longer accountable to the body, just as representation was no longer determined solely by an optical standard. Those prior standards, including the body's configuration, had assumed a sobriety and monumentality in discourse by the beginning of the twentieth century. One knows it is important to talk about a waist or about body symmetry, for example. But the Cubists were talking collage talk, the discourse of the vernacular and the seemingly unorthodox and unimportant, without the lofty, ponderous, and place-giving words of representation, worldly and bodily. Can we fault the new fashion designer for trivializing their enterprise, for deciding that the story would be lines, some patches, some swirls, and for refusing to talk about the profound matters of the body that every prior fashion designer of the West had addressed in earnest?

Collage implies a trivialization that is challenging, but it also categorically admits a vernacularization of the work of art that is similarly challenging to some. The century that Cubism created is also the century of news verbal and visual, violent and vile that runs from yellow journalism at the beginning to presidential scandal at the end (a second age for yellow journalism). But if Cubism permits art to embrace the ephemeral, the implications fall not only to a medium of newsprint to be included at will but also to fashion as a medium to be related to, at will. This does not mean, in the simpleton's solution, that one would seek every Sonia Delaunay and every drawing by Picasso indicating clothing but that one could imagine Cubism to allow and even to accept fashion as part of its larger principle of inclusion.

For, after all, Cubism described again and again a stylish world, emphasizing women who were sewing in counterpart to women reading and contemplating and women with fans in whose faceting and many indeterminate, changeable planes there was a paradigm for art's own creation.

There was a precedent to women sewing and women with fans; Cubism was not unique in those preoccupations—quite understandably, given the styles (including a romantic revival of eighteenth-century fans) of the 1910s and 1920s. But there is no precedent for the operation of the collage prepared as a paper (dress) pattern now documented, through which the process of the ephemeral and vernacular enter into art, not merely as an option of observation but as a process to be emulated and incorporated as well.

Cubism in fashion also wholly understood collage not only as the form of contemporary art but also as a "primitive" tradition, suggesting regional dress and the cutout forms that have been an important part of traditional dress, crude perhaps by sophisticated Western standards but nonetheless very much a part of regional costume. The multiple influences of Japonism, the Ballets Russes, and other exoticisms of the early twentieth century were clearly within Cubism's view and purview. Cubism's ready acceptance of the "primitive," exotic, and even regional in art corresponds to this interest evident in dress if not in collage. In the same measure that Cubist painters and sculptors were knowing naives, so too were the fashion designers.

Cubism's importance resides not in its iconographic invention but in its creation of new pictorial conventions. As fashion is capable of iconography—but more prone because of its expression on the body to pictorial and decorative determination—its ligature to Cubism is especially promising and easily could have been felt as early as the 1910s and 1920s. In fact, it was. In the December 15, 1920 issue, *Vogue* offered an article headlined: "The Cubist Lends Aid to the Costumer: The Parisienne Finds in the New Art A Clever and Modern Way to Decorate the Frocks of the Winter Season." Fernand Léger reportedly would visit Vionnet's studio to watch her working, fascinated with her technique. Cubism was neither sovereign nor exclusive by nature; relations to fashion as another visual art would be only natural.

Pablo Picasso

Woman in an Armchair, 1913

Oil on canvas, 58 ¼ x 39 in. (148 x 99 cm)

Copyright Christies Images, 1998

As the techniques necessary to collage entered the repertory of Cubism, the painting's image was uncannily influenced in a clear reversal of traditional hierarchies. To learn from collage is to affirm the power of the commonplace and the vernacular.

Pablo Picasso

The Aficionado, 1912

Oil on canvas, 53 ¹/₈ x 32 ¹/₄ in.

(135 x 82 cm)

Kunstmuseum, Basel

Copyright Giraudon/Art Resource,

New York

So engaging were the formal possibilities
pioneered by collage that painting could
not ignore the new ideas involved. In fact,
many of Picasso's paintings are grand
testimonials to collage, that supposedly
lesser, more ephemeral art form.

European

Two-piece ensemble, ca. 1920
Red silk with polychrome appliqué
Gift of Mrs. Louis Rorimer, 1938
(CI 38.2.18a, b)

While the specific vocabulary of this
ensemble with collage-like piecing and
stitching is regional costume, the new and
sanctioned artistic practice of collage may
well have encouraged the designer's
sensibility for the collage procedure native
to apparel. The manner of appliqué is
conspicuous, a sign of process in an epoch
when the process of making a composition
flat-on-flat was revered and exposed.

Albert Gleizes

La Equestrienne, 1916
Oil and sand on board, 39 ³/₄ x 30 in.
(101.8 x 76.2 cm)
Gift, Solomon R. Guggenheim Museum,
1937
Copyright Solomon R. Guggenheim
Museum Foundation, New York

That Cubism influenced arts of movement
such as film and fashion is only natural,
given the Cubist propensity to swirling,
excited, never-static forms, as seen, for
example, in this work by Gleizes.

Pablo Picasso
Woman with a Fan, 1908
Oil on canvas, 59 $^7/_8$ x 39 $^3/_4$ in.
(152 x 101 cm)
Hermitage State Museum, St. Petersburg

Among the fashion conventions prized by Cubism is the fan, which opens and closes in kinetic motion. It is specifically perceptible as an intimate accessory, but the opened fan can imply vast energy through its unfolding segments, just as Cubism's fragments always maintain their own energy field.

European

Evening cape (detail), 1920s
Black net embroidered with metallic thread
Gift of Broome County Historical Society,
1980 (1980.164)

Unabashed decoration, accomplished
fracturing and fragments, and an almost
literally transparent flatness chracterize
this unadorned evening cape of the 1920s.
Without a label, probably expensive but
not couture, the cape is the simplest kind
of nongarment, all but lacking shape itself.
But its elegant pattern suggests what
fashion could make using the license of
collage and the splintered eye of Cubism.

Pablo Picasso
Woman with a Fan, 1909
Oil on canvas, 39 ³/₈ x 31 ⁷/₈ in.
(100 x 81 cm)
Pushkin State Museum of Fine Arts,
Moscow
Copyright ARS, New York

This stylish woman with a fan—which
combines fan, figure, and environment
in delicate slivers—is paired with
a coat that understands the Cubist
fracturing of the plane.

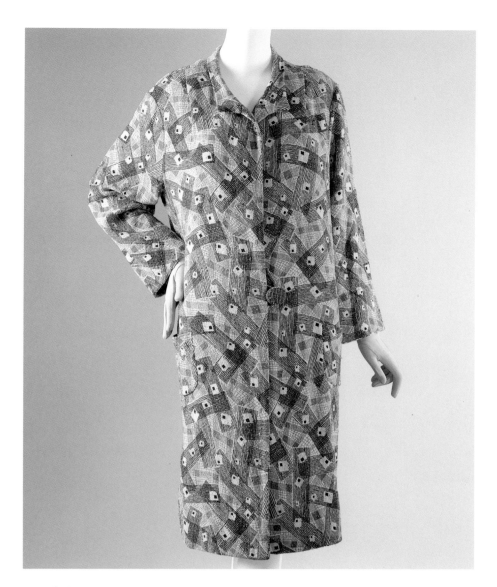

French/American

Coat, ca. 1926

White tussah silk printed with lavender
and black geometric pattern
Gift of C.J. Vincente Minetti, 1972
(1972.209.22)

Cubism's adumbrated geometry became
coin of the realm in the 1920s. Art Deco's
development of Cubism's selective
geometry into a wider array of shapes
carried Cubism as a pictorial taxonomy to a
much broader audience and wider appeal.

Jeanne Lanvin

Evening coat (and sleeve detail),
spring-summer 1927
Black cotton velveteen embroidered
with white wool
Purchase, Isabel Shults Fund, 1986
(1986.215)

From among the many strengths of Jeanne
Lanvin, it is her discriminating sensibility
for linear decoration that made her one of
the most important designers of the 1920s
and 1930s. Her starburst and radiant
designs were sui generis, though they
evoked the Art Deco style. As fashion
historian Caroline Rennolds Milbank
described her, "She seldom used patterned
fabrics, preferring to work with appliqués
and embroideries. Beginning in the teens,
she experimented with the modern look of
machine parallel stitching and, by the
thirties, was using lamé and satin worked in
parallel stitch and in honeycomb quilting to
form shoulder 'wings,' belts, and bibs on
otherwise simple columnar evening gowns."

Mariska Karasz

Day ensemble, ca. 1927
Navy-blue silk with appliqué of cream silk
Gift of Katherine J. Judson, in memory of
Jeanne Wertheimer, 1977 (1977.284.2a, b)

By the 1920s, American and French
designers were raiding regional forms of
dress. Ironically, that which Europe had
declared archaic and rustic only two
generations before in the face of the
juggernaut of modern industry and style
was now being recycled into that very
modern style and often held good claim to
the tenets that modern style prized. The
cutout flatness of Karasz's evokes Matisse
almost as much it does Eastern European
dress, its ostensible source. Karasz
understood the modernity of Cubism and
the Bauhaus well. She understood the
irony of placing motives of traditional
dress into a post-Kandinsky world.

Pablo Picasso

Queen Isabelle, 1909
Oil on canvas, 36 $^1/_2$ x 28 $^3/_4$ in.
(92 x 73 cm)
Pushkin State Museum of Fine Arts,
Moscow
Copyright Scala/Art Resource,
New York

Whether figure or design object, the
Cubist impulse was to float fragments and
pieces above and below one another on
an ambiguous plane, using the token
strategy of collage.

American

Evening pajamas, 1930s
Compound weave of gold, yellow, and black silk
Gift of Jacqueline Loewe Fowler Costume
Collection, 1981 (1981.149.9a, b)

Evening pajamas employ the same fabric
found in another Costume Institute
garment, shown on page 105. There are a
number of such instances in the collection.
What is striking in this case is that each
was anonymously designed into a garment,
suggesting the modern matrix of Cubism
perhaps tinged with Orientalism. In both
instances, the ideal is a kimono-like cloak.

American

Evening coat, ca. 1928
Compound weave of gold, yellow, and black silk
trimmed with brown dyed skunk
Gift of The Fashion Group, Inc., 1975
(1975.295.1)

When the same material as that in the
evening coat to the left turns up in another
evening coat (though not an ensemble:
only Hollywood would have put together
1930s evening pajamas and a fur-trimmed
opera coat), its Cubism-to-Art Deco
pattern takes on a robe-like drapery
reinforced by pagoda sleeves. In this coat,
there is a little bit of every modern impulse
in dress: Cubism, Art Deco, pattern,
Orientalism, and antitailoring. Yet, with all
its modern impulses, one can almost
imagine this coat (with less geometrical
pattern) worn by one of the Wise Men in
Northern Renaissance painting.

American

Day ensemble (jacket, shell, and pants),
mid-1930s
Polychrome dyed rayon crêpe
and red rayon crêpe
Gift of The Jacqueline Loewe Fowler
Costume Collection, 1996 (1996.135.2a–c)

As fashion in the 1930s moved through
Cubism to take on the enchantment of
leading modern architecture and design,
even a New York City skyline might
emerge from a pajamas day ensemble.

Juan Gris
Still Life with Bottle and Fruit, 1919
Oil on canvas, 29 $^1/_8$ x 21 $^1/_4$ in.
(74 x 54 cm)
Museo Thyssen-Bornemisza, Madrid
Copyright Nimatallah/Art Resource,
New York

In refusing verisimilitude as the objective
of representation, Cubism never stinted on
desiring observation. Objects and
observations were, however, to be
assimilated and transformed.

Modern Enterprises

Attributed to Gabrielle Chanel

Evening dress, ca. 1926
Black and gold metallic lace embroidered with
gold and black sequins
Gift of Mrs. Georges Gudefin, 1965
(CI 65.47.2a,b)

The overall view of the shimmering dress from which this detail is taken appears on page 121.

Cubism in fashion was indubitably late Cubism, as was Cubist theater, which was chiefly a reworking of the pictorial inventions made for fine art transferred to the stage. Neither Cubist fashion nor theater had a prime-cause experience similar to Picasso and Braque in about 1908–10. In fact, Cubism in fashion may have waxed even as Cubism in art waned in the 1920s and into the early 1930s. Derivative and/or diffusing, Cubism in fashion is nonetheless a genuine impulse of importance, even if not universally to the world of fashion. It was the cause of the central transfiguration of twentieth-century fashion at least until the 1960s, when the class structure and economic foundations of fashion were shaken and displaced by contradictory impulses toward art and the street.

Cubism in fashion involved not only those pictorial devices already described. It was a means for fashion to appear modern. It answered Poiret's great need to introduce new mechanisms to assure fashion's progress and change. His spectacles, his entourages, his licensing, his world tours were all part of an expansion of what Worth had done to establish fashion as a system. Poiret's contributions as merchandiser and impresario may prove to be the equal of his contribution as a fashion designer. He knew that fashion required creative and artistic partnerships and seized the vocabulary of art whenever possible to describe his ideas. His self-promoting autobiography, however, still could rank as a business plan for many in the fashion industry.

Even the more somber Vionnet understood there could be modern fashion without accompaniment by modern art and interior decoration. For the most part, the eighteenth-century styles that had prevailed for fashion interiors were replaced by the modern spirit, as into our time fashion repeatedly looks at modern design as a silent partner in the promulgation of fashion. Poiret would have it that he invented such ideas, but his usual myopic self-aggrandizement was at work. He had learned this lesson in large part from department stores and cognate merchandising. Their environments and their advertising were modern—think of S. Bing's propitiously-named "Salon Moderne"—because they knew the value of that mercantile "spin" long before it became political lingo. Poiret's shrewdness was tellingly modern: he saw the fashion designer as one who made the fashion but who also assumed significant responsibility for its consumption. Yes, Poiret always stood ready to exploit art to his benefit, and modern art in particular, but it was not only art that he chose. He was ready to line up any force he could to substantiate his enterprise in fashion. In a later instance, Chanel did likewise and continued to practice her media magic into the 1970s. Picasso, Braque, and other Cubists led us toward a similar model for the artists. Also into the 1970s, Picasso, in particular, worked at his reputation as assiduously as any artist in history.

The modern enterprise of fashion—and presumably that of art as well—is not only comprised of Promethean, life-changing innovations of the kind that Cubism produced in about 1908. As Robert Rosenblum has pointed out, even the first leaders had moved on as others moved into the pursuits and advancement of Cubism. Inexorably, the twentieth century has wanted to be modern. Fashion is, by definition, modern, and in philosopher Gilles Lipovetsky's argument it is one of the chief symbols of being modern, leading other arts and businesses. "Consumption as a whole now operates under the sign of fashion," Lipovetsky posited in *The Empire of Fashion*. Would that same perception have been true of fashion before 1908? Probably not. The unremitting sense of fashion novelty may begin with the generation of designers in this book, most notably Poiret, Chanel, and Vionnet. They made their lives conspicuously and controversially modern. They put forth fashion that could be highly controversial, and Chanel and Poiret even courted risks of ridicule in the garments they made. Perhaps the recourse they had to the fine arts was a natural affinity to the avant-garde, whether aesthetic or commercial. Today, we know that fashion leads the commercial avant-garde, appropriating many of the devices of the artistic avant-garde going back to the 1910s. The century and its avant-garde "Wheel of Fortune" turns and returns to its origins.

After all, these fashion designers were not playing it safe even as late as the 1920s. One cannot equate the first collages with the bias dresses of Vionnet or the sportswear proclivity of Chanel, but it cannot be forgotten that these now-venerated designers were themselves taking risks with the new. Fashion may be said to lead the new only because at times it genuinely does, with or without art. Neither art nor fashion realized Cubism in isolation; for both art and fashion, Cubism was just a part of being modern, but a necessary part.

Juan Gris
Pierrot, 1917
Oil on canvas, 35 $^3/_8$ x 27 $^1/_2$ in.
(90 x 70 cm)
Collections Mnam/Cci—
Centre Georges Pompidou, Paris

A planar Pierrot such as this one might
be compared with the Poiret trompe l'oeil
dress on the facing page , as both are in
the heritage of Cubist collage.

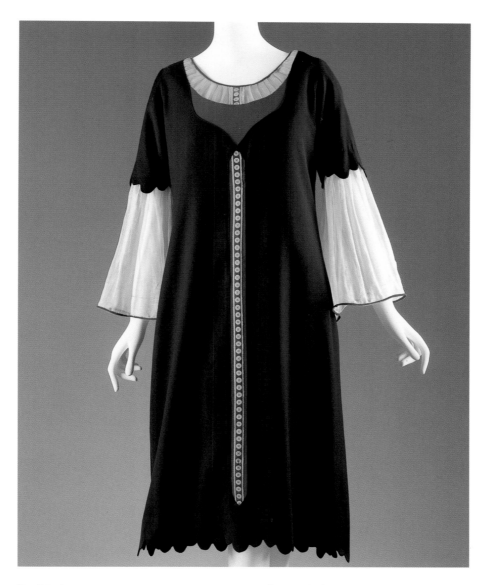

113

Paul Poiret

Day dress, ca. 1925
Navy-blue wool, red wool and cream silk
organdy
Gift of Mrs. Alfred Rheinstein, 1950
(CI 50.117)

In a very curious dress for Poiret, the designer builds around a placket of trompe l'oeil buttons in the manner of Cubist collage including real objects. Poiret's interest in art was lifelong. He wrote of his childhood, "I went constantly to the exhibitions of painting, and I sought to discover in them those who were going to be the masters of the day after to-morrow." It is hard to know if Poiret genuinely remained open to art, but he certainly professed a keen interest, especially in the new in art.

Pablo Picasso
Man with a Pipe, 1914
Oil and papier collé on canvas,
54 ³/₈ x 26 ¹/₈ in. (138 x 66.5 cm)
Musée Picasso, Paris
Copyright ARS, New York

There was, of course, a favored and
familiar repertoire in Cubist collage:
tabletop, musical instruments, women
with fans, men with pipes. These
accustomed subjects were especially
recognizable because of the frequency
of their appearance.

Juan Gris

The Book, 1913
Oil and papier collé on canvas,
16 ¹/₈ x 13 in. (41 x 33 cm)
Museé d'Art Moderne de la Ville de Paris
Copyright Giraudon/Art Resource,
New York

If rendered asunder by the new pictorial
ideas, the book on a tabletop is nonetheless
a referent to the integrity of the life of the
mind, contemplative and reflective.

Georges Braque
Woman Reading, 1911
Oil on canvas,
31 ³/₄ x 21 ¹/₄ in. (80.5 x 54 cm)
Private Collection, Basel
Copyright Giraudon/Art Resource,
New York

A reader seated in a comfortable armchair
becomes a mass of planes. Cubism's
recurring interest in contemplative
activities such as reading, smoking, and
sewing has been reflected in fashion's
creations for human participation in the
quieter aspects of life.

Fernand Léger
Woman Sewing, 1909
Oil on canvas, 28 ¼ x 21 ¼ in.
(72 x 54 cm)
Collections Mnam/Cci—Centre Georges
Pompidou, Paris

To the serene, world-knowing processes of
reading and contemplating, many would
add sewing, another activity of quiet self-
absorption. She who sews could be the
gender mirror-image of he who paints.

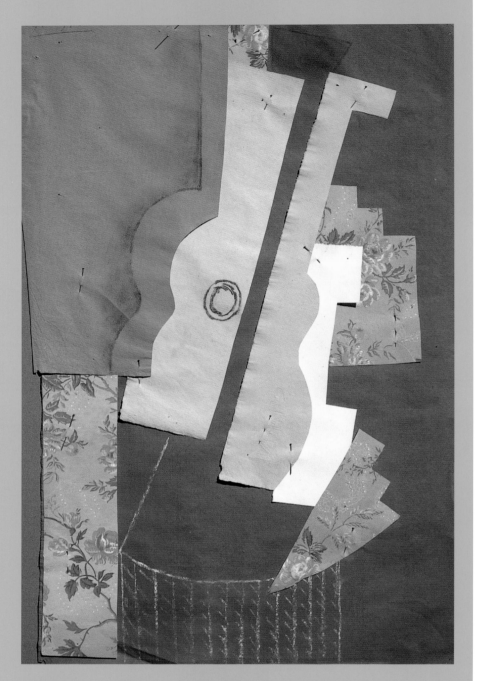

Gabrielle Chanel
Blouse, 1930-1935
Navy blue wool jersey with thin white stripes
Gift of Mrs. Michael Blankfort in memory of
her mother Mrs. William Constable Breed,
1976 (1976.29.7)

Chanel's "jersey revolution" was
characterized by the art historian Jean
Leymarie: "The use of jersey, which
harked back to her peasant childhood by
defying the conventions of luxury, called
for purer lines and created a revolution in
costume and appearance. As she herself
said: 'In inventing the jersey, I liberated the
body, I eliminated the waistline (which I
brought back only in 1930), and created a
new silhouette....'" The sports jersey was
all line and all movement.

Pablo Picasso
Guitar sur un gueridon, 1913
Papier collé, straight pins, and chalk
on paper, 24 ³/₈ x 15 ³/₈ in. (62.1 x 39 cm)
Private Collection

The pastiche of elements assembled into
collage that entered into the new pictorial
world was governed by rigorous rules,
despite an apparent informality bordering
on chaos. Correspondingly, the dress of
sportswear was softer and different from
prior dress but no less exacting.

Georges Braque
The Musician, 1917–18
Oil on canvas, 87 ⅛ x 44 ½ in.
(221.3 x 113 cm)
Kunstmuseum Basel, Switzerland
Copyright ARS, New York

The rich syncopation of pattern for a
Cubist musician, as exemplified in this
Braque, constitutes a synaesthesia in its
own right and represents the beauty
realized in the new pictorial stratagem.
The pattern of the evening dress on the
opposite page is highly reminiscent of
Braque's *Musician*.

Attributed to Gabrielle Chanel
Evening dress, ca. 1926
Black and gold metallic lace embroidered with
gold and black sequins
Gift of Mrs. Georges Gudefin, 1965
(CI 65.47.2a,b)

If there was a "jersey revolution," there was another revolution led by Chanel: the metamorphosis of metal into a malleable, knitwear-like form. Such metallic lace dresses were coin of the realm in the 1920s, using a vocabulary that merged Cubism with Art Deco.

European or American
Dress (and detail), ca. 1928
Black net heavily embroidered with silver and
black beads
Gift of Madame Lilliana Teruzzi, 1981
(1981.454.15)

The new soft dress had the capability to
dazzle. In fact, its soft surface was born to
shimmer and shimmy, defying the tradition
of apparel as carapace and affirming a new
premise of apparel as flattened, softened,
diaphanous lattice.

Lord and Taylor
Coat (two views), 1920s
Printed polychrome silk brocaded with metallic
thread and honey dyed fox trim
Gift of Jacqueline Loewe Fowler Costume
Collection, 1982 (1982.82.29)

By the 1920s, the geometries of Cubism
and later Art Deco had so fully
intermarried that many great coats and
capes might qualify as a late-effect Cubism.
This especially-good candidate reiterates
the rectangles with quilting.

Fashion Rendering

Thayaht
"Un Manteau, de Madeleine Vionnet"
(detail of page 134)
Gazette du Bon Genre, 1922

No one would be surprised that Cubism had an influence on the way fashion is represented, in both fashion photography and fashion illustration. Concerning the former, the specific effects were negligible, since photography was still coming of age for the fashion magazine and the considerable influence of artistic photography still prevailed. Concerning fashion illustration, the same Cubism that arguably constructed (and deconstructed) the forms of a previously representational fashion established new ways of seeing through the pictorial frame of Cubism.

Most importantly, the picture plane was fractured. Cubism's most easily imitated pictorial device was almost immediately taken up in fashion illustration. Graphically, fashion illustration as an abbreviating, essentializing system of notation had always eliminated or merely suggested some of the determinants of space and perspective with the assumption that these would be understood within pictorial convention. When Cubism offered another pictorial convention, the adumbrated forms of the illustration began to float in space and to take on the new, less gravity-prone aesthetic. In particular, high-style fashion advertising, including that of the house of Vionnet, accepted such a floating world. In this instance, the decision was not merely that of an after-the-fact illustrator; it was also an official sanction from the fashion house. Reticence made much fashion advertising very traditional, but no such timidity was observed by Vionnet, who perceived an integrity among all the expressive parts of the fashion house. Poiret would have claimed likewise, but his advertising image was far less progressive than his otherwise avant-garde styles and his novel uses of display and presentation.

Of course, it would not be long before the American fashion magazines would benefit from European modernism under the art direction of M. F. Agha at *Vogue* and Alexei Brodovitch at *Harper's Bazaar*. These two graphic designers understood that modern fashion could only be embraced within the graphic design of modernism. The elegance, simplicity, and energy that these magazines expressed in the 1930s was indebted to Cubism. These two popular magazines propagated not only the Surrealism that *Harper's Bazaar* so admired in the 1930s and 1940s but even more importantly, the reduced, abstracted forms derived from Cubism. We cannot imagine our modern fashion image without these magazines.

But Cubism went through important stages along the way, before it became so mainstream in design in the 1930s. Central in that period is the work of Thayaht (palindrome artistic name for Ernesto Michelles, 1893–1959). Thayaht seized not only Cubism's lashing line but its energy as well; he transformed the segmenting slices of a Cubist surround into the dynamic lines of force that would put a model into swirling motion suggesting an automaton of the runway. Thayaht's matrix in Futurism would explain the presence of these lines and vortex as well as the proclivity to motion; he never let fashion appear static but instead placed it within an implied energy field. Thus it was that Thayaht's sophisticated artistic journey, as associated with the fine arts as it is with the applied arts, influenced his imagery. That Thayaht placed his prodigious talent chiefly in the service of Vionnet was no small accident; he recognized the compatible sensibility and the possibility that he could suitably represent her work.

Thayaht was no ordinary illustrator. In fact, he saw himself as a fashion inventor with specific reference to his collaboration with his brother toward the development of a utopian system of clothing for men, which was issued as one of many Futurist manifestoes. Thus, a designer more than a subservient illustrator, Thayaht conceptualized illustration. As much as his lines of forces suggest motion and eternity in the utopian forms of clothing that included asymmetrical vests and jackets for men with Futurist prints, his 1920s illustrations for Vionnet suggest at least an exalted ephemerality for fashion. Vionnet dresses shown with twists and complexity are often difficult to identify in illustrations; Thayaht's illustrations are especially perplexing and suggest a generic rather than a specific similarity. How ironic that some of Thayaht's most effective images depict the sports of golfing, swimming, and skating that capture real motion through Cubist devices. These are not Cubist or Futurist masterpieces or the kinds of fashion that will foster a more perfect, utopian future. They are therefore perhaps less than Thayaht's highest aspirations. They are merely the most practical form of fashion and lifestyle. They became lifestyle images precisely because Cubism was by the 1920s able to achieve lifestyle.

But Thayaht was not alone. Fashion illustrators selectively borrowed from Cubism, coveting its association with the progressive and modern and responding to its uses of the part to indicate the whole that fashion illustration had always known as a principle. Cubism was a second-generation presence for fashion illustrators, entering that realm only in the 1920s, long after the first wave of Cubist invention. But Cubism would be destined to maintain a long presence in illustration and in graphic design, a fashion not utopian but one that would last for decades to suggest style, sports, energy, and the new in synthesis.

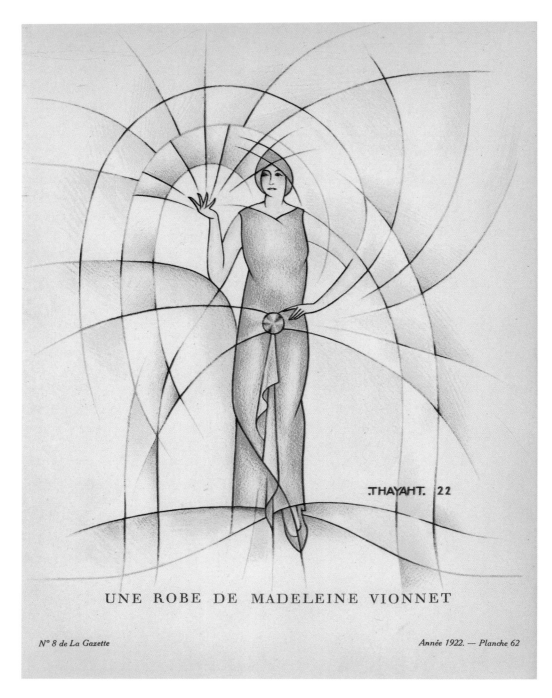

UNE ROBE DE MADELEINE VIONNET

Nº 8 de La Gazette

Année 1922. — Planche 62

Thayaht

"Une Robe de Madeleine Vionnet"

Gazette du Bon Ton, 1922

Thayaht
"Souvenir de Paques à Rome"
Gazette du Bon Tòn, 1922

AUTOMNALE

TAILLEUR, DE MADELEINE VIONNET

N° 4 de la Gazette.   Année 1923. — Planche

Modèle déposé. Reproduction interdite.

Thayaht

"Automnale"

Gazette du Bon Ton, 1923

POUR LE GOLF

COSTUME, DE MADELEINE VIONNET

N° 7 de la Gazette.   Modèle déposé. Reproduction interdite.   Année 1924. — Planche

Thayaht

"Pour le Golf"

Gazette du Bon Ton, 1924

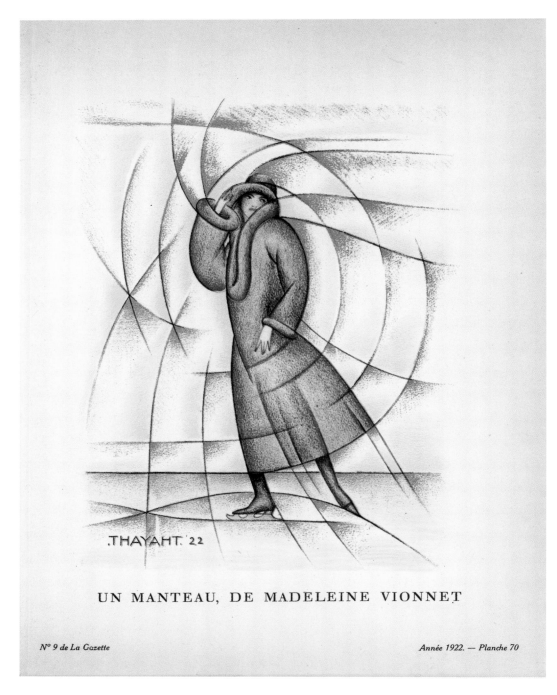

UN MANTEAU, DE MADELEINE VIONNET

Thayaht
"Un Manteau, de Madeleine Vionnet"
Gazette du Bon Genre, 1922

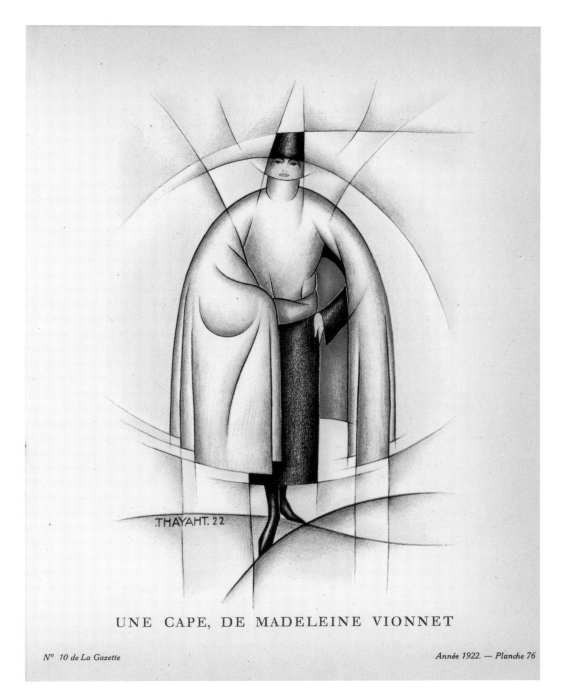

UNE CAPE, DE MADELEINE VIONNET

Thayaht

"Une Cape, de Madeleine Vionnet"

Gazette du Bon Ton, 1922

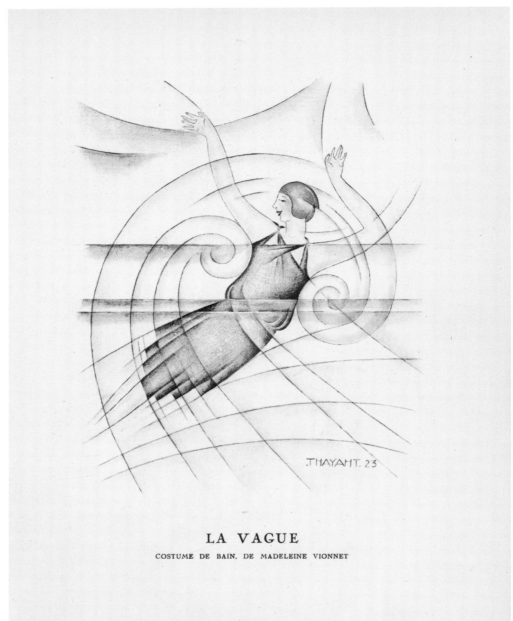

LA VAGUE

COSTUME DE BAIN, DE MADELEINE VIONNET

Nº 3 de la Gazette.   Modèle déposé. Reproduction interdite.   Année 1923. — Planche 11

Thayaht

"La Vague"

Gazette du Bon Ton, 1923

PENDANT LES "MODÈLES"

CHEZ MADELEINE VIONNET

Nº 3 de la Gazette du Bon Ton.

Année 1922. — Planche 20

Thayaht

"Pendant les 'Modèles'"

Gazette du Bon Ton, 1922

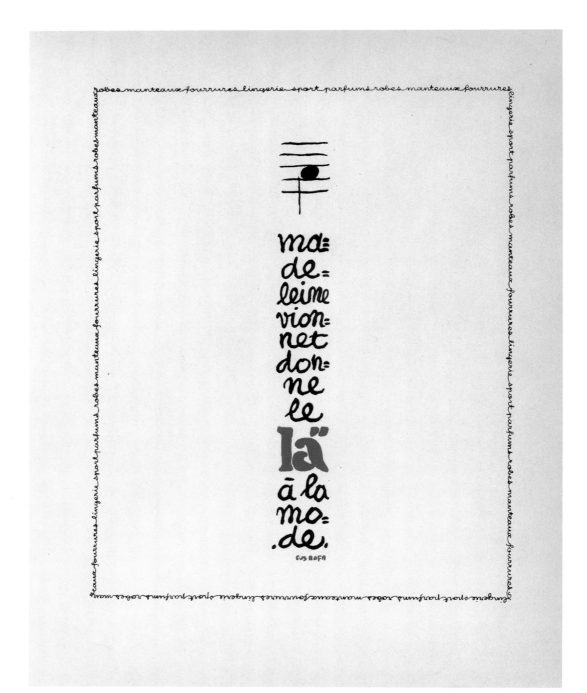

Gus Bofa

"Madeleine Vionnet, donne le Lä à la
Mode"

Pan, Annuaire du Luxe à Paris, 1928

RELATION

MANTEAU DE SPORTS, DE PAUL POIRET

N° 1 de la Gazette du Bon Ton.   Année 1921. — Planche 6

Charles Martin

"Relation"

Gazette du Bon Ton, 1921

LA DERNIÈRE LETTRE PERSANE

Extrait de l'Album édité par les Fourrures Max

Gazette du Bon Genre. — Nº 10   Année 1920. — Planche 73

Iacovleff

"La Dernière Lettre Persane"

Gazette du Bon Genre, 1920

BAINS DE MER

parfois des oiseaux, il nous consolait de penser que par des chemins invisibles, cette première nuit qui allait tomber sur Loti laissé du monde, un concile de petites mortes se réunirait peut-être pour lui apparaître enfin avec des visages

76

Giron
"Bains de Mer"
Gazette du Bon Ton, 1923

Lucien Boucher

"Modes Agnès"

Pan, Annuaire du Luxe à Paris, 1928

Albert Gleizes

Woman with Animals (Madame Raymond Duchamp-Villon), 1914

Oil on canvas, 77 ^{5}/$_{16}$ x 45 ^{15}/$_{16}$ in. (196.4 x 114.1 cm)

Solomon R. Guggenheim Museum, New York

Copyright Solomon R. Guggenheim Foundation, New York

The evidence of a shared vocabulary of angles and planes in Cubist art and Cubist-inspired design was not as broadly circulated as later correspondences between Surrealist art and graphics were. Because Cubism's influence on graphic design was strictly limited to high-end design, it seldom reached popular culture, as Surrealism so often did.

Madeleine Vionnet

Day dress, 1926–27
Maroon silk crêpe
Gift of Mrs. Aline Bernstein, 1945
(CI 45.103.2)

An intersection of pin-tucked seams
functions both as fragmenting line and
assembling structure in this Vionnet dress.
Nothing more, or less, gives shape in this
soft dress, in which the pin tucking
provides the transition between an
uninflected bias bodice and a box-pleated
skirt. The delicate lattice is the essential
structure of the dress, gibing all form and
shape. Of course, it exemplifies form as
function, a modern tenet seldom tested
against but paramount in Vionnet.

Henri Matisse,
Portrait of Yvonne Landsberg, 1914
Oil on canvas, 58 x 38 ¹/₂ in.
(147.3 x 97.8 cm)
Philadelphia Museum of Art: The
Louise and Walter Arensberg
Collection

One of the great portraits of the
twentieth century is, of course,
uncannily like—and prototype for?—
Thayaht's brilliant fashion illustrations
of the following decade (see cover and
pages 130 to 137).

Persistent Cubism

Christian Francis Roth

Dress, spring 1991

Pieced polychrome cotton sateen

Courtesy Amy Fine Collins

The interconnecting shapes of planar geometry that obtained in Cubist art of nearly a century earlier predominate in this detail of the Roth dress shown on page 150.

Cubism has persisted. Although its major accomplishments were articulated during the first decade of the century, Cubism has remained a pictorial system viable through at least half the century and vivid throughout the nearly one hundred years since its inception. Robert Rosenblum wrote in 1960, "Yet, if the generative power of Cubism has waned, the authority of its major statements has not. The cardinal works of Picasso and Braque not only take their places beside the masterpieces of the Western pictorial tradition but offer standards of twentieth-century achievement by which the art of today and tomorrow will be measured." Rosenblum's strong statement for Cubism as a distinctly twentieth-century art and reckoning can also encompass its broad outreach into areas such as fashion. To speak of a "persistent Cubism" is not to say that Cubism has retained its very brief dominance; it is to say that it has entered the pictorial vocabulary never to be entirely absent again. We have all become Cubists as a function of living in the Cubist century.

For fashion, the evidence is particularly strong. Cubism is the device by which fashion was flattened; it will always be remembered in any era of flat dresses. The most recent era of flat dresses was the late 1960s: Courrèges, Cardin, and paper dresses all testified unequivocally to the obvious forms of Cubism, promoting an overt geometry, often banal, in dress. The quintessential dress of the era was Yves Saint Laurent's "Mondrian" dress, just slightly displaced art-historically from the flatness of Cubism.

About the persistence of Cubism one argues for the continuity of a visual language, not for the excellence of each example, though some revivals are always of import and fascination. As abstraction and representation, each crudely defined, oscillate in twentieth-century art, so too do the claims for flatness of fashion and the three-dimensionality of fashion-trade authority back and forth over time. Cubism is both the original (in the West) and the most compelling argument for flat fashion, and so interest in it is rekindled with each turn toward the flat. That flatness is also easy for fashion: not every geometric textile design for a dress is a return to Cubism. Extraordinary embroideries derive from the initiatives of Picasso, emphasizing the plane but also enjoying fashion's innate fancy and extravagance. Yet, it is hard to say that this art selection is anything other than predictable at the end of the century in which Picasso has been seen as one of our most heroic artists.

On the contrary, it is those designers who think again in the mode of Cubism who verify its true persistence and potential for expanded presence. Thus, Rei Kawakubo's wrapping and twisting, obviating front and back, may be a sign of the original Cubism, even as it is taken on as a late-century enterprise. For Geoffrey Beene, the influence is Vionnet and the possibility of the sheer plane that circumnavigates the body as he does, gently with lace inserts, ridges, and gentle incisions. Especially important to the innovative designers are the twists of Vionnet, defying fashion's conventions but also letting a little three-dimensionality flex its way onto the flat field of dress. Indeed, such fashion designers as Ronaldus Shamask and Yeohlee have been chiefly identified with the hard arts of architecture vis-à-vis fashion, but they might be more comfortably accommodated by Cubism as a soft, easy art of modified representation apt to fashion and its humanism. Further, such soft notes define the humanism of long-term Cubism. Christian Francis Roth takes his blocks and cylinders from the colorful vocabulary of Sonia Delaunay. It is not an idle invocation of art as a striving for fashion that prompts these various unnamed and hard-to-describe efforts at a supple planarity, for they are, in fact, never equated with Cubism and seldom with art. Rather, these are genuine efforts at the end of the twentieth century to see how fashion yet unfolds and how fashion embraces us.

Picasso once said that his work is his diary. One can modify that aphorism to know that Cubism is the twentieth-century's diary, personal and perennial.

Christian Francis Roth

Dress, spring 1991
Pieced polychrome cotton sateen
Courtesy Amy Fine Collins

Roth has set himself the task of simulating in dress virtually every important period of art history. Cubism is no exception; his blocks and planar overlaps capture the spirit of the art. Of course, Roth (b. 1969) is a latecomer; he was born some six decades after the origin of Cubism, yet he, too, remembers.

Pablo Picasso,
Seated Man, 1917
Oil on canvas, 41 x 21 ³/₈ in.
(104.2 x 54.2 cm)
Museu Picasso, Barcelona, Spain
Copyright Giraudon/Art Resource,
New York

Ultimately, Cubism depicted things and people. What is common between people and things? the objects of apparel, of course.

Art
and
Fashion

Bergdorf Goodman Co.
Cape (detail), 1914
Black silk satin with black silk fringe
Gift of Mr. Andrew Goodman, 1954
(CI 54.26)

This shimmery black detail highlights the silk satin and the fringe of a 1914 cape shown on page 156.

A hundred years ago, the relation between art and fashion was sought in the like sensations of a synaesthetic world. Of late, we have been prone to link art and fashion through the issues of body, gender, and identity that are key to contemporary art and equally crucial to contemporary fashion. But neither poetry nor polity makes the equation work. One is right to be skeptical of the supposition that art and fashion are made of, animated by, or heading toward the same aims and criteria. Fashion is irrevocably commercial; its system is somewhat different from the system and culture of art.

Ironic it is that the conclusion to this book seeks to refute the expectation of art and fashion in tandem. We have, in fact, been assaulted of late with a politically correct and intellectually irresponsible claptrap that art and fashion should be mingled and merged, at least on the plane of exhibition. Then, curators and would-be curators show us the usual suspects, which invariably include a few utopian tokens of fashion or a few crossover works by artists making clothes, and then we are reminded of recent art, especially by women and gay artists, in which clothing constitutes a significant metaphor for the body. Insulting in the echelon of their fallacies—from the ridiculous premise that an object of clothing is the same as fashion itself through the misunderstanding that artists may experiment with a variety of forms and media and ending with the mistake that all of art history is to be determined solely by the contemporary—these reasonings and these exhibitions that slash together art and fashion are profoundly unworthy

Installation view of the exhibition
"Yves Saint Laurent," The Costume
Institute, The Metropolitan Museum of
Art, December 14, 1983, through
September 2, 1984.

and only repeat outmoded concepts and ludicrous categorizations. If anything, such exhibitions do more to disprove the art and fashion ligature than they do to prove it.

If there is ever to be an art and fashion connection, it must be founded in another level of understanding. We must appreciate that art springs from deep motivations. Art desires to reform perception and/or culture. Let us say then that at the core of Cubism is not its repertoire of pictorial devices but its urgent sense to re-order and reconceptualize the pictorial process for the twentieth century. Without accounting specific devices, this fundamental one might well be shared with fashion, and that is the premise of this exhibition and book. Deep roots make connectors, not flimsy filaments of after-the-fact pseudo-morphisms and trendy likenesses in tempo. If Futurism and fashion are connected, they are held together at the political root, in their wanting to see all of culture changed. If fashion and Surrealism are in some way tethered, especially in popular culture, it is not in mere resemblance but in the will to engage the emotional and psychological in lieu of a representational verity in modern culture.

Fraught as it is with misapprehensions, the art and fashion connection is the bane of the costume curator's professional life. No other suggestion save showing Hollywood costumes or, more recently, Princess Diana's dresses is more frequent or more vehement. Everyone says, "Why don't you do an art and fashion show?" To my succinct answer, "never," some do not hesitate to reply, "Well, you could do it

Installation view of the exhibition "Yves Saint Laurent," The Costume Institute, The Metropolitan Museum of Art, December 14, 1983, through September 2, 1984.

your way." I've done it my way: NO WAY. The generalization is inane and not even worth consideration. Do not, under any circumstances, use this book recklessly; do not believe in art and fashion simply on the evidences of some select relationships in one art movement. The three fundamental unities I pose—flatness and the presence of the cylinder along with the plane, denial of "representation" in its accustomed Albertian or volumetric space, and the indeterminacy of forms—are there to be accepted or rejected, perceived in Vionnet and Chanel, established in Picasso and Braque, nowhere wholly documented, nowhere proved other than as evidenced in the works. This is not an exhibition that proves itself with one tattered fashion drawing by an Old Master or a fashion designer's baleful remark that he or she wished to be an architect. The joining of art and fashion cannot be so loose and so rootless. You have to believe in the immensity of art, its full compass, its compelling example to every human being, and especially every visual person. If art and fashion are conjoined, it is because of the magnanimity of art, its big spirit for all things created. Cubism was munificent and bountiful, and fashion responded with alacrity and in ways that also could impress any viewer with their grandness, their fearless will to change, their complete transfiguration of dress along with a twentieth-century view of the body within dress.

Art and fashion. Two powerful cultural elements. Seldom in unison, though perhaps here, beneficially so, through the radiant ingenuity of Cubism.

Bergdorf Goodman Co.
Cape, 1914
Black silk satin with black silk fringe
Gift of Mr. Andrew Goodman, 1954
(CI 54.26)

Chic, amorphous capes of the teens such as this one could continue to instill the old rigid silhouettes, but they also accommodated new possibilities for apparel soft and cleaving to certain planes of the body.

Pablo Picasso,
Woman in a Black Hat, 1909
Oil on canvas, 28 ¹/₂ x 23 ¹/₄ in.
(73 x 60.3 cm)
Toledo Museum of Art, Ohio; Purchased with funds from the Libbey Endowmant, Gift of Edward Drummond Libbey, and Purchased with funds from the Florance Scott Libbey Bequest in Memory of her Father, Maurice A. Stott

The stylish portrait, once in the domain of a Renaissance optic, could be achieved in the twentieth century only when style and art came under the aegis of Cubism and its newly articulated form of beauty.

Acknowledgments

I owe Robert Rosenblum an immense debt of gratitude for *Cubism and Fashion*, though he may well reject such appreciation as a liability. I read *Cubism and Twentieth-Century Art* early in the 1960s and later heard Robert lecture on "The Typography of Cubism" at Bryn Mawr College in 1965. I was convinced by his large view of Cubism, then rare; what I had seen as optic became in his brilliant insights an unfolding, still vital cultural phenomenon. Robert's ideas of an expansive Cubism have stirred me for a long time. In the mid-1980s, I wanted first to do *Fashion and Surrealism*, but determined that "one day" I would follow it up with *Cubism and Fashion*. So, after some twenty-five years of my malingering and eleven years of vague intention, I quickly thank Robert Rosenblum. Though they were spared for the most part from the first thirty or more years of that odyssey, I am nonetheless indebted to the staff and friends of The Costume Institute who have suffered with the zeal of *Cubism and Fashion* in its last, most intense stages. Their criticism and creativity and unfailing support have done far more than my dawdling to make this exhibition and book: Janie Butler, Anne Byrd, Deirdre Donohue, Michael Downer, Minda Drazin, Lisa Faibish, Ellen Fisher, Rochelle Friedman, Dorothy Hanenberg, Barbara Havranek, Stéphane Houy-Towner, Jennifer Kibel, Alexandra Kowalski, Marilyn Lawrence, Emily Martin, Chris Paulocik, Bonnie Rosenblum, Birdie Schklowsky, Rose Simon, and Judith Sommer.

Just as important as those who have already given themselves to

Cubism and Fashion are those in The Costume Institute who get to do what I would most love to do: spend the coming four months living with and working on the exhibition. I know that Kitty Benton, Barbara Brickman, Nancy DuPuy, Eileen Ekstract, Julie Duer, Susan Furlaud, Betsy Kallop, Susan Lauren, Butzi Moffit, Victoria Munroe, Wendy Nolan, Pat Peterson, Christine Petschek, Dee Schaeffer, Nancy Silbert, and D. J. White will teach me more on this subject in the next four months than I learned in my procrastinating thirty-five years.

Other effort and assistance within The Metropolitan Museum of Art has been generously given by Richard R. Morsches, Emily K. Rafferty, Linda Sylling, Barbara Weinberg, Michael Batista, Jill Hammarberg, Zack Zanolli, Karin Willis, Elyse Topalian, and Bernice Kwok-Gabel. Beyond the Museum, I am most grateful for special assistance with *Cubism and Fashion* to: Geoffrey Beene, Beverly Birks, Marion Greenberg, Titi Halle, Martin Kamer, Rei Kawakubo, Betty Kirke, Christian Francis Roth, Connie Uzzo of Yves Saint Laurent, Ronaldus Shamask, Emanuel Ungaro, Patrizia Cucco of Gianni Versace, and Yeohlee.

Of very special note and deep gratitude: John P. O'Neill, Takaaki Matsumoto, and Barbara Cavaliere made the book I dreamed about. John's wondrous encouragement, Takaaki's unstinting patience, and Barbara's editorial partnership continue to make beautiful books where, by all rights, none should exist. The book you hold, like many before, I owe entirely to them. I am ever indebted to Philippe de Montebello who indulges me in my ideas and rewards me with his.

Richard Martin
Curator, The Costume Institute,
The Metropolitan Museum of Art

159

Celant, Germano. *Art / Fashion*. New York: Solomon R. Guggenheim Museum, 1997.

Cowling, Elizabeth. "The Fine Art of Cutting: Picasso's *Papiers Collés* and Constructions in 1912–14." *Apollo*, 142. November 1995, pp. 10–18.

Daix, Pierre, and Joan Rosselet. *Le cubisme de Picasso; catalogue raisonné de l'oeuvre peint 1907–1914*. Neuchatel: Ides et Calendes, 1979.

Daix, Pierre. *Cubists and Cubism*. Translated by R.F.M. Dexter. Geneva: Skira; New York: Rizzoli, 1982.

Delaunay, Sonia. *Sonia Delaunay, Art into Fashion*. New York: Braziller, 1986.

Gaya Nuno, Juan Antonio. *Juan Gris*. Barcelona: Ediciones Poligracia, 1985.

Golding, John. *Cubism: A History and an Analysis, 1907–1914*. Cambridge, Massachusetts: Harvard University Press, 1988.

—*Georges Braque*. London: Knowledge Publications, 1966.

Hayward Gallery. *Addressing the Century: 100 Years of Art and Fashion*. London: South Bank Centre, 1998.

Kahnweiler, Daniel Henry. *The Rise of Cubism*. Translated by Henry Aronson. New York: Wittenborn, Schultz, 1949.

Krauss, Rosalind. *The Picasso Papers*. New York: Farrar, Straus and Giroux, 1998.

Martin, Richard. *Fashion and Surrealism*. New York: Rizzoli, 1987.

Rosenblum, Robert. *Cubism and Twentieth-Century Art*. New York: Abrams, 1966.

Rubin, William, (ed.). *Pablo Picasso: A Retrospective*. New York: The Museum of Modern Art, 1980.

Schwarz, Arturo. *The Complete Works of Marcel Duchamp*. New York: Delano Greenridge Editions, 1997.

Vriesen, Gustav and Max Imdahl. *Robert Delaunay: Light and Color*. Translated by Maria Pelikan. New York: Harry N. Abrams, Inc., 1969.

Selected Bibliography